T0349101

THIS ALL

THIS ALLOTMENT

THIS ALLOTMENT

Stories of growing, eating and nurturing

Edited by Sarah Rigby

Elliott&Thompson

First published 2024 by
Elliott and Thompson Limited
2 John Street
London WC1N 2ES
www.eandtbooks.com

ISBN: 978-1-78396-788-9

Permissions:
Page 75: Jenny Mitchell, 'A Man in Love with Plants' from *Resurrection
of a Black Man* (Indigo Dreams Publishing, 2022). Copyright © 2022
by Jenny Mitchell. Used with the permission of poet.
Page 189: 'This Allotment' from *The Heeding* by Rob Cowen
© Rob Cowen, 2021, published by Elliott & Thompson, reproduced
by kind permission of David Higham Associates.

Picture credits:
Page viii: Sarah Rigby © Sarah Rigby; page 6: Kirsteen McNish © Kirsteen
McNish; page 28: Olia Hercules © Joe Woodhouse; page 42: Heather Leigh
and David Keenan © Heather Leigh and David Keenan; page 58: Marchelle
Farrell © Penny Wincer; page 74: Jenny Chamarette © Ellenor Benton of Yellow
Bird Photography; page 100: Rebecca Schiller © Jared Schiller; page 120:
JC Niala © JC Niala; page 132: Alice Vincent © Alice Vincent; page 138:
Sui Searle © Sui Searle; page 154: Tony Scott, Newburn © Peter Fryer;
page 170: Sara Venn © Sara Venn; page 188: Rob Cowen © Paul Crowther.

9 8 7 6 5 4 3 2 1

A catalogue record for this book is available from the British Library.

Typesetting by Marie Doherty

Printed by CPI Group (UK) Ltd, Croydon, CR0 4YY

CONTENTS

A BEGINNING

Sarah Rigby

'Where did it begin?' somebody asked me recently. 'This love of gardening, this allotment, where did it start?' I found it hard to answer. It's an urge that takes so many of us – to grow, to tend – but an allotment holds a unique allure, a quality all of its own. It's different to the connection I have to my frost-cracked pots at home, or to the community project where knees meet soil alongside professional growers and other volunteers. I realised then that I wanted to understand this feeling better, through the eyes and the hands of other allotmenteers with their own relationships with these places – and the idea for this book began to grow. Through their writing, perhaps I might catch hold of an answer to that question of where this all began for me.

Was it my sister with her own allotment that sparked this urge? Was it when a friend asked me if I wanted to try to grow something on the back of a neighbour's patch when our children were still small? Or during lockdown when the school's plot suddenly became wild, available, in need of tending through those months of hard and difficult things that felt like stones rather than seeds in my pockets. Was it the smell of my grandmother's tomato plants in her front porch, never used as an entrance but only to offer those tangy fruits light and warmth? Maybe it was the apples, peaches and damsons-thought-to-be-plums in my parents' garden, which each year provided a new flush of slightly bruised produce to sit on the drainer ready for coring, stewing, freezing. Or even further back? An ancestor, perhaps, with a tiny cottage garden on a Danish fjord growing leeks and herbs or on a Scottish hillside digging hard-won potatoes.

This question of beginnings – of where it all started – is something that comes up time and again in this collection, and it's the grandmothers, it seems, who frequently plant the first seed: for Kirsteen McNish in her grandmother's greenhouse; for Marchelle Farrell in her grandmother's burgeoning garden in Trinidad; for Olia Hercules in her grandmother's Ukrainian smallholding full of flowers. Yet you'll find the allotment 'old boys' here too, no fear: in care-filled nostalgic conversations with historian JC Niala; in the 'peaceable kingdoms' of Newcastle's allotment gardens recorded by Graeme Rigby, and in their stern-but-kind (or sometimes just downright stern) guidance for newcomers.

Wherever it began for me, this allotment, on which I sit making voice notes in September 2023 having recently commissioned these pieces, has bits of me tied into it now. There is, as Jenny Chamarette explores in 'Land Is the Work of Many Hands', an intimacy in coming to know a place. There's no letting it go. As for so many of the contributors you'll find here, I'm not sure I could make the break, even if I wanted to. Because allotments get under our skin. With splinters from woodchip and thorns from brambles, with compost under our nails and streaks of mud across our forehead for the walk home. Once we're hooked, they are places to which we cannot help but return, sometimes in challenging circumstances as in Rebecca Schiller's piece, 'Allotments Are Anomalies', sometimes because – as Sara Venn describes – they have become such a fundamental part of who we are.

I'm cutting back tomato plants as summer ends. For the first time, there's a chill in the air this morning that says the sun might be shining today but autumn is very much on the horizon. I'm picking a few final fruits too. Blight is taking parts of them now, but after hundreds and hundreds of yellow-red pops of acidic sweetness, is it any wonder these plants are ailing and that the soil needs mulching? There are spiders everywhere on the plot, weaving their webs, building their own places of sustenance and shelter among the yellowing fennel fronds. Yet, as the grasshoppers chirrup, perhaps for the last day this year, this place whispers that a new growing season is not far away. This time will come again. The beginnings of it are already here.

As we'll see in David Keenan and Heather Leigh's beautiful conversation, there is a sense of time unfurling at different speeds on an allotment. Ten frozen-handed minutes becoming a morning-long winter woodchipping session. Long, languid summer afternoons turning into evenings that hang in the balance. Of circular time, where the rituals of a new growing season come back around each year – the seed sorting, seed compost and seed trays (toilet rolls for sweet peas); the planting out, the covering with fleece or net; the building of pea frames as hawthorn blossom appears, the dismantling of tied-cane wigwams before the storms. And so the year turns.

In the distance, I can hear children playing in the park over the hedge, parakeets screaming across the marshes, distant aeroplanes buzzing. Allotments are so often places that are set apart, on the edges of a town or village, a railway, a road. They are vulnerable, their existence frequently threatened, as we'll see. Yet these places mean so much more than the courgettes, the marigolds and the tumble-down structures that some might imagine could just be picked up and relocated, grown again elsewhere. They are full of life. Community, yes, as we'll hear in Alice Vincent's 'Space to Grow: Women and Allotments'. But also rocket flowers buzzing with bees, shield bugs in the raspberries, fungi and microbes and roots working in symbiosis – ongoing 'frenzies of birth and death', in the words of Rob Cowen, that make allotments some of the most ecologically diverse places in the country.

We are, as Sui Searle underlines, 'intimately interdependent'. We rely on these many interconnected relationships for our survival, for our joy, for our sense of ourselves. For in the blackcurrant bushes already producing leaf buds for next year, the tender new chard waving in a slight breeze, the ants nesting in the compost bin, the dock emerging from the bed again, the smell of a ripening tomato for a kitchen table, in all these things, we find a sense of home. Because the land welcomes us back. There is always a new beginning to be found here – a sense of something half forgotten pushing back through if given half a chance.

September 2023, February 2024

FAIL, REPEAT,
BEGIN AGAIN

Kirsteen McNish

My first hazy memories of seeing produce grow are down to my maternal grandmother. She lived in a post-First World War house in Nottingham, a typical semi-detached on an estate cul-de-sac, with a front and back garden and an outside loo. My grandma was a petite, twinkly-eyed woman, who would laugh a lot; warm and quick-witted. I remember her almost always with her half-pinny on, cooking from scratch, retrieving things from a small larder. She was very house-proud, scrubbed her step and swept every day, but prouder still of her garden, graced with a greenhouse and a stubbly grey concrete path leading to a vegetable plot.

In the hazy recollections of childhood, my sister Rachael and I would create dance routines in that garden, pretending to be on *Top of the Pops* and bickering about who did the steps best. In the amber glow of the early eighties, we would stay there for a couple of weeks each summer with her and my two youngest aunts. My grandmother would do handstands against the stippled rendered wall with Rachael and me, and in the evenings we would watch *Tales of the Unexpected*. Lights off, she would dance in front of the fire, mimicking the silhouetted dancer of the show's opening credits, making us collapse in giggles until the programme got too frightening, and we were hurried off to bed with the hallway light on, whispering to each other in the dark.

In the daytime, however, it was this glass house of Grandma's that entranced me. Sneaking in, the sharp fresh smell of tomatoes turning from green to red and warming under glass, mingled with the almost sickly sweet smell of earth nestling cheek-by-jowl with crescent-moon, bumpy-skinned, odd-shaped cucumbers. Here was twine to run between my fingers and make cat's cradles, mucky gloves to wear like Frankenstein's monster as I chased my sister, a leaky iron watering can with tape on the handle, tins with the labels taken off holding emerging seedlings. I would shower the watering can back and forth over the vines, making the smell headier – breathing it in deeply.

In the late afternoons, we would kneel on chairs in the kitchen shelling peas while Grandma sliced potatoes and runner beans that smelt as fresh as newly cut grass. This garden was also where my mum had played as a child, and looked after her younger siblings when she wasn't doing chores, and when we visited they would murmur the flowers' nicknames together as they walked around the garden before we set off for home in Corby – a place she never settled. Busy lizzie, forget-me-not, baby's breath, love-in-a-mist and bleeding hearts; the words comforted and soothed her. It was up behind the greenhouse, however, that felt like a Narnia of sorts to me. Obelisks of sticks with climbing runner beans with scarlet hermaphroditic flowers, sweet peas, garden peas, lettuce, cabbage, cucumbers and nasturtiums. The remaining details have evaporated into the vagaries of time, but I remember running to this patch in the rain once, so pleased to have been sent out for something for dinner and with the special responsibility. When I asked my father recently how big the garden was, he told me it was half the size it held in my imagination – such was its dearly held part of my youth.

My mother inherited a love of growing from seed from my grandmother. We would often see her, creative at her core, building cold frames and a makeshift greenhouse of sorts from offcuts of wood and cheap plastic sheets. Pinch pots were made from compressed newspaper (almost nothing was wasted). She was ultra-resourceful but in an age of the heady spread of supermarkets, she never branched out into vegetable or allotment patches. And with eight active children, footballs, bikes and second-hand tennis rackets, she perhaps thought better of growing things that could be so easily, if unintention-ally, destroyed. Like my grandmother, as she worked she wore an apron, which once held a tiny, almost hairless abandoned kitten, nursing it back to health against the warmth of her chest. Planting out seeds, her tongue tip always curled up to her top lip in concentration. With a locked-away basket of tough memories and present-day worries, her garden was her respite and escape from pain and worry. We weren't encour-aged to get involved. To grow and nurture quiet things was a place of survival in a life that hadn't always given her an easy ride.

Not long before she died, my mum had a nasty fall in the garden. My dad was impervious to her calls, listening to football on the radio as she lay for at least an hour in the dewy grass. I imagine that to feel so vulnerable in the place she loved best, and where so many of her strengths had played out, must have been a heavy blow. In the last weeks before she died, she asked every day to be taken to the window to see her rose bush – in the wheelchair she resented suddenly having to use. I have seen the garden she created only once since, but the neat, organised rows in her shed and the cold frames leaning against the back of the house remain still, legacy pieces of her toil.

*

My first flirtation with growing and allotments comes in my early twenties, shortly after graduating. I'm living in Hull in a flat whose road is wide and regal – rows of trees set alongside beautiful, opulent-looking Victorian buildings – sectioned off in mini roundabouts by old fountains and tall statues. Many bohemian folk live here and I'm sharing a top-floor flat with my musician friend Jez while recovering from ME after glandular fever had swept through my body. My friend D visits to see how I am doing. She has a waspish energy, like an unattended hosepipe thrashing around, and unless she's stoned at the end of a night out rarely do I see her still. Restless as a storm, her body athletic and chiselled, she paces around my living room, then leans out of the window to have a cigarette. On the exhale, she tells me she now has an allotment, and I break into a smile. I cannot imagine this charismatic heart of the dance floor bent over with a spade tending veg. With a withering look, she stubs out the cigarette butt on the windowsill and tells me that she has made friends with her allotment neighbours (all retired). She loves sharing cups of tea and cake with them and learning about their lives: one allotmenteer had given her purple broccoli and peas for dinner that she said melted in her mouth. Admonishing my smile with a sideways look and a flick of her long dark fringe, she suggests that getting an allotment might be good for my recuperation. I should get in touch with the council for a plot.

Not wanting to disagree with her formidable forthrightness, I do what she says.

For a few pounds a month, I am soon offered a plot on Chanterlands Avenue Allotments near the disused railway line. I arrive on my ancient sturdy Dutch bike, but I can't see D anywhere. An elderly man asks me my name and laughs, gesturing at the sunglasses perched on tip of my head. 'Ooh, come from the French Riviera, have you?' he smirks, but leads me to my patch. He tells me that I can ask the council to rotavate it, 'just the once for free, mind, and then it's just you and elbow grease'. He introduces me to a neighbour and he in turn offers me a bottle of dusky home-made wine as a welcome. Another shows me his abundant flower patch with hundreds of bobbing daffodils. I feel both welcomed and slightly intimidated. I have never really considered what I eat or the seasonal connection with any weight. In the whirlwind of socialising, working and going to gigs, then illness, everything I buy is from Jacksons Stores, quick to cook and abundant all year around. Through one shed's window, I spy a hand-drawn chart of what will come up when and times to sow; spidery drawings of flowers and veg done in fine black pen alongside motifs for the seasons, an artwork in itself.

I go up to the allotment each week as much as I can planting in higgledy-piggledy rows that resemble unravelled knitting. In time, the tops of carrots begin to poke through and the mangetout start to wrap their soft tendrils around rigid canes. I am comforted somehow by the fact that as I work I know that there are potatoes nestled warm under the earth. My input varies according to fatigue, and some days it's enough just to sit and watch the birds. I am intimidated by the abundance all around me: flowers, scarecrows lurching on poles like drunks at a bar, mosaics made from beach-found glass shimmering in the sun, driftwood mobiles and bottle tops clanking merrily in the breeze. This haphazard community – a contrast to the rows of neat houses just a skip away – seems to reuse and repurpose so much, and joyously so. I am happy here alone, fudging it all, with benevolent smiles and greetings from others, whole generations and lives lived distinctly apart – but communing here.

One day, not too many months after my allotment dabbling begins, my sister visits from Leeds and I have a bike accident after not the brightest move: a pizza box balanced precariously on my handlebars to take home for tea. A teenager darts across the road in front of me and I brake too hard and hit the deck with my legs still entangled between the crossbar and the wheels. A speedy hospital visit and then weeks of hobbling ensue. When I do get back to my patch, I find it in a state of undress. Everything has shrivelled through lack of water, been pecked at or is bolted and leggy. My potatoes are the only hardy, stoic survivors. It's an overcast day to match my mood and for once there are no other growers there to share my dismay. I decide to hand my patch back to the municipal authorities and admit defeat, tail between my bruised legs.

In 2017, my sister dies suddenly from an innocuous sore throat, which turns rapidly into sepsis. Not realising that she is becoming gravely ill, she tends to her ailing children. She leaves us on an early evening in March, close to what would have been her birthday and Mother's Day. In the ensuing days, weeks and months I feel as if I am falling down a well every time I shut my eyes and try to sleep. When I wake, for a few dewy split seconds I forget that she is gone until the pain comes screaming through me raptor-like once more. I bookend the days gazing at the blank green expanses of my garden lawn in the early light, and again last thing at night, trying to figure out in the darkness how someone I loved and knew all my life simply doesn't exist any more. I feel guilty as I don't live near her young children, the eldest about to sit his GCSEs, the youngest a tender four years old.

Aside from planting numerous sickly coloured selections of flowers from a DIY chain and demolishing some badly built, cracked old cement troughs, I have not really been bothering with our city garden. Yet one day, months after my sister's death, I am wandering around by the trees, unable to rally myself, and touch the heavy bowing blossom heads of an elder. My brain tells me that Rachael will never know that I am here doing this, and I immediately feel ludicrous as it's not a thing I would ever have reported to her. Yet this simple impossibility burns everything down and suddenly I am lost again, at sea. My chest seizes up and tears storm my cheeks like liquid released from a shaken bottle. I decide then to bury my hands in the earth.

The next day, my young son and I arrive at the garden centre where I head for the young plants, not yet confident enough to grow from seed. I reach for peas, courgettes, runner beans, tomatoes; he chooses strawberries and pumpkins, anticipating the intense thrill of a Halloween to come. We arrive home and I assemble click-clack flower beds, thinking of my sister who was devoted to her brood but also supported me from afar with my disabled child. Despite her shyness, Rachael would always reach out to elderly neighbours and run their errands, would always support me with my daughter. That she will never grow into middle age herself sends pains into my breastbone as I pat down the earth. That done, my five-year-old boy merrily proclaims that 'now we have a vegetable garden!', enthused by the illustrations he's seen in his Richard Scarry books. My daughter sits close, playing with the remnants of the compost from the bag, sifting it through her fingers like rubbing pastry, utterly absorbed. Once the weather warms and the produce springs into action, a tortoise-shell butterfly often flits around and lands on my son near the beds. I think of my sister's long pale fingers, as delicate as its fragile wings.

Within weeks, we see stealthy runner beans creeping up a wigwam of canes, and after a couple of months we are joyfully picking peas and strawberries and placing them into bowls with pride, admiring our small teatime crop. Despite assur-ances that courgettes are easy to grow, they haven't made an appearance, and we never quite manage to grow a pumpkin in which to carve crooked teeth. The next year, we collect a rescue kitten from a sanctuary on the Holloway Road and she starts using the beds as a litter tray. I remove the surrounding soil, spray citrusy water as a deterrent, put up nets, but soon the squirrels follow suit, digging furiously to bury their hoard. I feel defeated. My son loses enthusiasm. The canes remain in place, totemic for a further few months, yet even they are eventually pulled down and replaced by white anemones, ferns, grasses, driftwood brought back from the coast sticking out at strange angles and scarlet poppies thrilling the eye for their transient and glorious days. Every now and then, small juicy strawberries appear to give the birds or insects something to nibble at. A tortoiseshell arrives again the following summer and each year until we leave, flitting around the willow tree, landing on my son's sleeve or sometimes on my daughter's amber-streaked chestnut hair. A reminder, perhaps, not to forget how fragile things can be.

After eight years in our East End borough, and twenty overall in the city, we decide to turn things upside down and move. With the 'tired of London, tired of life' maxim hovering over me like a neon sign, and all the clichés of moving to the country in middle age ringing, it is something rather different that motivates our relocation. It is becoming ever harder to navigate the city with a growing disabled child. She is often over-stimulated and there are few places to take her safely without overcrowded public transport being involved. After an extensive period of shielding her during the pandemic and a lack of childcare support, we are collectively exhausted. My son too has been crushed by returning to an unsympathetic teacher who doesn't understand his dreamy forgetful nature and my partner has had an unexpected health scare, enough to shake him and keep him awake at night. In the cruel short days of early January 2022, my mother died a harrowing death after a short but scarifying illness in her early seventies. And so, against all odds and after a hard battle as banks start to close their doors to new mortgages, we somehow slip through and sell our little house with its beloved garden. We buy another in Devon by the skin of our teeth, to go back near to where my partner grew up.

On one of our last days in the city, I sit with my friend Madeleine in her allotment behind the leisure centre drinking tea as she too prepares for a move, in her case overseas. A gallery professional, ceramicist and vibrant conversationalist, she is shaping up her plot for her successor, the growing season nearly over. Birds in the hedgerows chatter shrilly and the watery early September sun warms our heads. We discuss the fears around our respective upheavals, the leap into the unknown, the impact on our kids and partners. Both of us have worked for a long time in the arts and have no connections or jobs to go to – but go we must. I stretch languidly like a cat as I get off the allotment chair and imagine the expanse of Dartmoor spreading before me in its autumnal bracken, lichen and peaty waters – my chest rises in giddy anticipation. Our new house will be buried deep in a hamlet at the foot of Dartmoor's moody hills and hers in the mountainous ranges of southern France. She hands me three plants and some soft fruit to take home, and we squeeze each other goodbye in solidarity. I am aware of the town clock chiming three peals in the distance, and within three weeks we shall be waving goodbye to this home in Walthamstow, its marshes, green open parks, allotments and beloved friends.

*

We arrive in Devon and I immediately want to grow something. I want to put down physical as well as emotional roots. Yet planning anything is made almost impossible by the sheer amount of renovation needed to make the house watertight and by the fight to get a suitable school place for my daughter. I panic that time is running away and a strong current of adrenalin courses through my body as I decide to try to create a patch *right now*. I need to anchor myself to something outside the house. I dip into Charles Dowding's *No Dig* book, mulching the red earth with the rotting hay and compost I have to hand and hastily planting redcurrant and blackberry bushes, kale, cabbages, cauliflowers, potatoes, pinky-red chard. Between the rows, I place the large flattish stones I have dug up from the earth, creating a pathway that curves like the crescent moon that's hanging over me as I finish, parched and filthy. I am deliriously happy out here; alone and glad of it.

The hamlet in which we've found ourselves is largely a farming community. On our lane there are nine houses, in four of which live farmers, up at the break of day and working valiantly into the night, tractor headlights on most days of the week. Some work for other farmers or landowners, others rent land for their livestock or have their own spaces on the curvilinear green hills. Most of my neighbours stop to chat regularly at the front gate, or we wave or nod heads in the early hours when it seems too indecently early for words. One farmer has an allotment next to the ancient well that we can see from our kitchen window, which yields him an enviable amount of produce, including sweet peas by the bunch that he sells in a little roadside box, common here but which I still find surprising and somehow magical. In the blazing heat of late May he invites me onto his patch to show me his bounty. The cauldron-like vat in which he stirs his secret-recipe plant feed takes my breath away with its fetid potency.

On my regular pilgrimage to the village well, I peek at his wooden bench laden with marrows, beans, flowers, gourds and more sweet peas, shining in the light like a harvest festival offering in a seventies magazine. In my own south-facing plot on the hill, the heat is fierce and affords no shade. I water by hand as best I can in the thick of a hosepipe ban after weeks of relentless sun, but it never feels quite enough. I manage to get some red chard and one purple cabbage into a roast dinner, but then the rains come again thick and fast, as do a great many caterpillars, who claim residency on my patch (or what's left of it). I speak to Madeleine in the mountains of France, and she too has lost three-quarters of her crop. As we chat, buzzards mew low over the fields and a sparrowhawk screams from the trees, swooping down to scoop a mouse in its talons. Two majestic peregrine falcons have also arrived in the hamlet for the first time in years. I wonder if the extreme weather is offering them little of abundance also. I am well suited to planting a garden in the spirit of creative disorder and experimentation, but realise that if this is going to work then I am going to need some guidance.

I meet Robyn from Outside on a day heavy with low-hung milky-grey skies that make you feel as if there is a seal on the world. As I arrive, rooks spool in the merry-go-round of clouds skittering across the hills into the valley below, the winds coming in strong from nearby Bantham Beach.

Outside is a space that seems to join communities living in this part of Devon effortlessly. It has a beautiful shell-shaped skate bowl, a ceramics studio, a café and a bounteous field that houses an allotment and polytunnels. I squint at the allotment garden as Robyn beckons me into a no-nonsense cabin lined with practical sterling board. She speaks quickly with knowledge and warmth, an electric contrast to the dull day. She explains how she runs the kitchen gardens here in response often to the requests of the head chef in the café, Joe, and is occasionally helped by the odd volunteer. She tells me about her working patterns tuned to the seasons, of trying to balance the quantities they need for their dishes, which soft herbs can be grown alongside quicker wins such as mangetout, radishes, chard, salad rocket and chicory. As Robyn speaks, she conjures a layered tapestry of produce that grows joyfully in my head. I ask how this project has been affected by the burgeoning climate crisis and she explains that 2023 has been incredibly challenging: the coldest spring in six years, the hottest June on record, the wettest July. Yet this plot is bursting at the seams, fecund and popping with colour. I sigh as I think of my own withered space on the hill.

As we chat, I watch the last of the summer's swallows loop low, butterflies blown off course by the sudden bursts of wind. I can almost taste the nearby sea on my lips. We go headlong into talking about the work of the writer Lucy Jones and the teachings of gardener Alys Fowler, the impact of relationship breakdowns, grief, ancient approaches to the land, the impact of loss on a cellular level and how getting on our hands and knees and feeling a deep connection there allows the earth to respond in return. The synergy between Robyn and this place is evident. There is more to learn here from her than I ever could from a guide to growing.

I quickly relay my failings, explaining how I raced ahead trying to start a patch in late spring, breathlessly asking which crops I can grow into autumn. I want easy insights. Quick fixes and success. She smiles and stops me in my tracks by asking how much time I can realistically expect to spend on an allotment every week with my caring and work responsibilities.

Rather than dampening my ardour, this gentle question immediately gives me permission to plan something that needs less
attention than my disabled daughter, to work within my means.
She suggests more hardy veg such as kale, onions, leeks, and
crops that will grow perennially, including fruit bushes. For
our strong Dartmoor winds, she suggests windbreaks that I
can make myself. But for now, she says, just observe. Look
at where the shade is, where the water pools, where the frost
pockets sit, where the wind, sun and dry patches develop. I
can put cardboard down until spring, letting the soil sleep,
letting the plot reveal itself to me so that I might try to intuit
what it needs.

She advises me to count how many earthworms are present, to roll the soil between my palms to get a sense of its
structure, to consider whether it might be boron or calcium
deficient. I tell her a neighbour has offered us horse manure,
but she explains that she favours green manures such as
buckwheat and fenugreek; complementary planting including clover, chicory, trefoil and nettles. Veterinary treatments
are often present in traditional manures, she says, which
could affect the plants and are generally more polluting.
She thinks from my description of the earth on my patch
that the soil is likely to be compacted: learning to be patient
and observant is key; analysis rather than quick flirtation is
what's required.

The longer-term aims of the team at Outside reveal a bursting seed pod of ideas: they will create several permanent no-dig beds, build their own large-scale compost system, add 70 metres of willow hedging for coppicing once established. There will be an edible perennial forest hedge, a mushroom crop in the dark and dank area behind the cabin, new perennial crops such as saltbush, sea buckthorn and other coastal plants, and a sensory area designed for neurodivergent children who prefer softer spaces. At this point I struggle to push back tears. It is potent to feel that children like my daughter are tangibly seen and considered as part of the fabric here.

Robyn tells me that while gardening can be a solitary endeavour at times, engaging in outreach work with their community is very rewarding, including a project called 'Seed to Loaf' with a group of eight-year-olds from a local primary school. They are taking part in the entire process of making bread from the first sowing of the seeds through each stage of harvesting, threshing, winnowing, milling and baking. Robyn was fortunate to have access to a 'population wheat' called Mariagertoba. Unlike the commonly grown monoculture wheats, where each grain is genetically identical, Mariagertoba is a community of diverse varieties that can cross with each other and year on year become more diverse, more adapted to the land it's grown on. Diversity is the key to this wheat's resilience, and it requires no herbicides, pesticides or fertilisers to thrive – it's been bred to grow in organic conditions. Robyn regales me with how once the ground was prepared she gave the children a pouch of seed each, explaining that 'now you need to press it onto the soil by hand, to walk it in or even dance it in'. And how every child chose the last option – a silent, joyful wild-stepped disco. Later, she and the class then worked with a regenerative community-interest company called 'Till the Coast Is Clear', who helped the kids and their families harvest the wheat by hand, threshing it by bashing it wildly in pillow-cases – a great moment of hilarity and release; stress relief for the parents letting go too. These images strike me deeply – a layered yet largely invisible process that most of us don't see or understand due to produce just appearing on shelves in front of us without question, such is our privilege and dissociation with how growing and the subsequent produce works. Outside is the antithesis of all that: a place of connec-tion that pulses from the moors to the sea with purpose; that aspires to engender a sense of gathering, communing, wider understanding and care towards others and the environment; and also a place of joyful sharing and respite.

I pad around the polytunnel with Robyn. Cosmos at its entrance bursts like fireworks as we step in; mugwort ceremo-niously flanks the curves of the opening, offering a protection of sorts. Inside the aubergines look almost unreal, suspended on vines, resplendent, jewel-coloured and unbloated by enhanced feed. She hands me a tomatillo and it bursts in hints of melon and cucumber on my tongue. The last of the cherry tomato crop hangs in sculptural shapes from a hanger suspended from the tunnel's ceiling while tangerine French marigolds dance in the narrow slant of light at the end of the tunnel. To my side, Padrón peppers hide under shiny deep-green leaves and large orange squash hang from vines waiting for their turn to be harvested. It feels full of promise. As I watch the light filter through the leaves, I am back in my grandmother's greenhouse, senses alight.

Outside, I walk through an abundant bustle of chard, carrots, mixed and rocket salad, nigella, chives, spinach, kale-ettes, many shades of chicory and swaying wheat stalks. Enormous veiny deep-green and purple cabbages stand close to leeks upright in rows of which a sergeant major would be proud, observed by sunflowers with faces as wide as dinner plates. I spy a composter – the Ridan – the size of a gym horse and filled with kitchen scrapings, sawdust and fine woodchips.

Later, back home, I text Robyn to thank her. And suddenly what I learned from our time together connects to the garden of my childhood like a new bead threaded on string: nothing in fact has gone to waste, including all my failures. In my patch that awaits my toil and my observation, I consider how we shall have to increasingly flex with resilience and creativity in a burgeoning climate emergency. In a world that craves homogenous perfection, and has little room for mistakes or difference, I value the quiet contemplation of my daughter and how she listens to her surroundings better than most, and how much we can actually learn from those who walk to a different beat. I want to embrace afresh what I see and sense, to learn to fail and then begin – again.

SOIL AND SONG

Olia Hercules

Ukrainians have thick black soil running through their veins. For a long time, Ukrainian language, traditions and folklore, including strong melancholy songs, developed and flourished in the countryside: the soil and the Ukrainian identity have been forever intertwined.

I was born in Kakhovka, a small town in the south of Ukraine. People often think of Ukraine as a cold place, but it is a huge and diverse country: woods and marshland in the north, mountains in the west, and open steppeland in the east and south, hot from May to October.

Chornozem, literally 'black soil', is some of the most fertile in the world, especially in the south. Back at my mum's house in Kakhovka, I remember finding a little tomato plant growing out of the cracks of the paved pathway to the house. You drop a seed – it grows and thrives, fed by the humus and stretched by the sun.

Our foods were colourful, varied, season-led. Everybody grew something, either on a neat strip of land circling your house, on a smallholding if you lived in the village or at allotments clinging to the edges of the city. Seasonal was the only option available for a long time; it was part of our lives – simple, sustainable living. I can still remember the smell and taste of the very first June-harvested cucumber, my mother thinly slicing it over a bowl filled with radishes, tomatoes and, of course, that Ukrainian staple: dill. Dressed with a spoonful of thick crème fraiche called *smetana*, it was pure magic. Flavours that still fire up my synapses, opening a portal into a world of love, beauty and comfort.

My Ukrainian grandmother, Lusia, had a smallholding. Lusia grew a lot of flowers. She sang and talked to them gently to help them grow. 'How are you today, *dorohenka*, my dear?' she would say, and then sing one of her favourites, about the war, the many wars. '*Ridna maty moya* . . . Dearest mother of mine, tell me why you aren't sleeping? Why you woke me to gaze at the stars up above? Did you know I was leaving? Tell me why . . . was that why you were grieving, was the cloth that you gave me a sign of your love?'

Like the embroidered cloth she sang of, stitched with ornate stems and birds, she marked her borders with splashes of colour, blooming flower heads everywhere, standing guard over the ground. Lusia especially loved chrysanthemums, peonies and asters. She also had her famous 'vitamin C row', as she used to call it, black and pinkish white currants and raspberry bushes. She grew her potatoes in a separate allotment, as aesthetically she thought that they made her plot look too bare before the leaves began to push through. Even in exile, these potatoes grew well and they tasted outstanding. Their flesh was so creamy that when boiled they didn't need butter, just the merest sprinkling of salt. Without trying, she passed on her love for home-grown produce to my mother.

Mum grew gigantic tomatoes, enveloped in bright-pink leather jackets that seemed to be bursting at the seams; mauve, rotund aubergines and peppers; dill and coriander plants with their airy parasols. There were trees too; trees were important. Peach, plum, sour and yellow cherry, quince, apricot and walnut.

This cornucopia of produce and knowledge might make you think that I was a seasoned grower from childhood. Yet I was never taught how to grow vegetables or to cook when I was growing up, though it would one day become my profession. My family believed that these things would naturally happen later, when I was an adult. If I had been more curious, I am sure that they would have encouraged me as they did with other interests, but I wasn't. When the USSR broke up, we felt we were behind, that a more traditional way of life belonged firmly to a time we were now pushing beyond. Life became fast and busy. We emigrated. We learned a new language and culture. We assimilated. There was no time or urge to sing, no place to grow the vegetables of home.

And so I was a late bloomer when it came to all three: growing, cooking, singing. But when that need came – and I can't explain it as anything else but an intrinsic need, a passion – it came to me fully and forever. This all-enveloping desire was suddenly there, but Lusia was long gone. And, aside from the songs she had sung to her plants, the melodies of which still floated into memory, I had no idea how she achieved anything so amazing as her garden and her table while raising six children.

I think part of this longing was the need to reconnect with home. I came to the UK when I was eighteen and, soon enough, felt a niggle that I didn't have the vocabulary or wisdom to name. I was having fun, studying and being independent, but something always felt a bit off. Only later, in my mid-twenties, did I realise that I was homesick, missing my family and the comfort of home-grown and home-cooked food.

I moved to London after I finished university in the Midlands, and it was here that I discovered the English allotment. There was one very close to my rented flat in Muswell Hill. Where Ukrainian allotments were borderless, flat, expansive, these English allotments were somehow full of detail, cosier in their patchwork form. I visited and was instructed to send a letter with a request and my email address. I received a letter back saying that I would have to wait a decade. My heart sank, but I asked to be kept on the list.

So much changed in the following years. For one, I moved six times, further and further away from my first London flat. The week I set up home with my new partner, Joe, in his place in East London, a good hour away by public transport from Muswell Hill, an email came through. Congratulations, it said, would you like that allotment? It was so far, but I could hear Lusia's singing coming from below the ground. Besides, I was lacking those dill umbrellas, an essential ingredient for all the brine pickling I was undertaking, so I accepted and prepared for long commutes. The plot, 10B, seemed ideal – not too much shade – but it was overgrown and neglected. I did not know where to start. My parents had lied: this knowledge I was supposed to have found as an adult was nowhere to be seen.

Lusia had only ever had one prized gardening book. Books were a deficit in the USSR, like everything else. I was lucky to have social media at my fingertips, and kind people that were so keen to help. Where do I start, please, allotmenteers? I received advice from many seasoned allotment holders.

I bought books and quizzed friends. Two very simple pieces of advice stuck: improve your soil, then stick seeds in it.

I contacted as many farms as possible looking for organic manure, eventually finding the well-fermented stuff in Wales. Soon enough, a man called Tom Jones, I kid you not, dropped bags of precious muck on our doorstep. I spent afternoons at the allotment with Joe and my four-year-old son Sasha. It felt so good to have them both there, for Joe to consolidate his love watching me ruddy-cheeked shovelling shit and for Sasha to connect with a garden. He ran around with a magnifying glass, watching epic battles between ants and caterpillars, spotting and naming spiders as we did at his grandma's in Ukraine, his chubby hands covered in soil. I thought I'd learn and that as I was learning I would teach my son. No need to wait for him to grow.

We found huge pieces of iron in the ground, boulders, bits of welding. The allotment had been established across abandoned railway tracks, the layers of land and history not caring that we now called it something new. There were also a lot of carpet pieces laid on the surface, which we threw away, not realising that these offcuts had been placed to suppress weeds, to warm up the soil in preparation for planting in the spring.

I wanted to be as kind as possible to my soil and the life within. I did not want to disturb it, devastating the critters and organisms that make up the soil. But we did lightly dig in the manure to begin, vowing to leave it be in the following years. With the ground prepared, I could now start thinking about growing the things I loved from Ukraine: herbs, especially dill, sorrel, horseradish and lovage – bunches of which I could not easily get in the shops. I also planted the vegetables that I fell in love with in the UK, things that were easy to grow such as chard and kale and land cress.

While we all toiled, I was singing to someone for the first time in years. Of course Sasha had heard me sing numerous times, but Joe was new in our lives, and I felt vulnerable. Joe immediately said my voice was good. I told him about Lusia's methods, about my family history, and he told me his. We fell so deeply in love; we got hitched within six months. We were writing a new tune into this land.

I had made a good 10B, but our spring holidays were looming and I wondered how the plot would fare in our absence. When we visited Kakhovka the previous summer, I had asked my mum for her cucumber and pattypan squash seeds, bringing them back to London in the zipped compartment of my wallet. Now, with Sasha's help, we filled trays with soil and stuck the little seeds in place, perched against the French door in the kitchen, surrounded by my giant ficus and huge monsteras (I love a jungle inside and outside). The seedlings grew to our squeals and songs. The day before we left for

Ukraine, for our Easter holidays, Joe and I headed up to our allotment to put them into the ground. We scattered seeds there too – sorrel, borage, nasturtiums and purslane; we were following advice to plant everywhere so that the weeds couldn't get through.

I have learned that with gardens and allotments, there is always a sense of foreboding if you have been away for any period of time. There is the wondering whether anything will have grown; the possibility of it all having been eaten by birds. Will the snails have feasted on anything green and edible? Will new seedlings have dried out and died? When we eventually returned and went to our plot, I looked with half-open eyes, thinking that there would be a tangle of weeds, ravaged crops, but I needn't have worried. It was huge with borage, chard, horseradish and rhubarb leaves looming over delicate, sprawling nasturtiums. It was wild, but it was beautiful. Then life became busier and busier, my career suddenly shooting off with a second cookbook deal and lengthy research trips in the Caucasus. Soon we were preparing to go to Ukraine, as we always did, for the month of August. We collected allotment bouquets for friends (chard, kale, nasturtiums and sorrel) and left.

We returned to a menacing letter from the council warning us that unless we tidied up the plot it would be taken away. I hadn't managed to make strong enough connections with my allotment neighbours to ask them for help *in absentia*. To be honest, I didn't know what the standards were. We couldn't imagine this place that we had so lovingly revived being removed from our care, so in shock we hurried down there. I suppose there was a point to be made: the summer had created a wilderness out of control. To me it didn't look uncared for, though. It certainly was not the plot I inherited – all overgrown impenetrable brambles and tall weeds. I thought ours, even though unravelled, looked good for the bees, but perhaps those with the say-so felt we did not visit often enough, and we lost 10B.

In 2017, we moved house again and there was a small garden at the back. The lawn came out immediately and Joe put in some wooden planks for me, creating new beds. I planted more of the same: lovage, chard, sorrel, dill. I did make the mistake of not enriching with manure first, forgetting the first of those simple pieces of advice. And many of the things I planted did not make it in the heavy, claggy clay. People said they were surprised I managed to grow anything at all with an old eucalyptus tree towering above, that great sucker-up of water and nutrients.

Yet the first year was the best. The courgettes were bountiful. I didn't even plant the pumpkin on purpose, just threw some seeds out for the birds in the autumn, and in the spring a strong plant grew and sprawled out of the borders and towards the kitchen door, presenting us with four perfect pumpkins. Cavolo nero was delicious; we had so much chard, I started pickling it. The peas flowered bright purple; the cherry tomatoes were sweet, if a tad woolly. The kale burst out in amethyst leaves and kept us fed for a good six months until it bolted. The cucumbers were bitter, the broad beans covered in aphids. I decided I had to pick my battles, and grow plants that were self-sufficient.

Again I wanted herbs, lots of herbs. My mum grew six types of basil in Ukraine, and I yearned for at least a fraction of that bounty here. Mammoth dill did well at first, but I have not been able to grow it again since that first year. I bought little plants of Vietnamese coriander, pineapple and chocolate mint, planted sage and was gifted an oregano and marjoram plant. All of those are still thriving, almost an all-year harvest, even in December. Every year I plant tagetes and marigolds among them. At the end of the season, I cut off big clumps of each and hang them upside down on the ceiling of my kitchen – a bit of witchery and magic for warm cups of herbal wintery tea.

In early spring 2022 my plot was bare. I was preparing my seeds, just as my mum was in Ukraine, and then the unthinkable happened. Ukraine was invaded by Russia, atrocities committed in our home town, and my parents were forced to flee. FSB officers moved into my parents' home. We don't know how the garden is doing. They blocked the road, so remaining friends cannot even come close enough to peek behind the fence. For a long time, it was hard enough to get up and start the day, forget sowing seeds or cooking soup.

Two years have passed now since the big war started, and the situation hasn't changed, an area the size of Germany is mined, my parents are still in exile, and missiles keep raining onto people's homes and land. But Lusia's singing from below the earth is getting louder, reminding my mum and me that life must prevail whatever the circumstances, however hard and heartbreaking. When we saw each other last, for New Year 2024, we all sat around the table and sang 'The Red Guelder Rose' from our land.

I read somewhere that research has shown that plants love the vibrations that come from our singing. And I know for a fact how good both the vibrations of plant-growing and song are for humans too. In 2019, when I was pregnant with my younger son Wilfred, I read somewhere that singing engages your lizard brain, and that when that primordial part of you is activated, it makes the process of giving birth feel less painful. And so a few months later, during a planned home birth, I sang as Wilfred was born. Not necessarily deliberately, it just felt good to make deep guttural sounds, I sang-shouted Ukrainian folk songs, full of powerful, loud wails. The birth wasn't completely pain free, but it was a good birth. And my urge to sing grew and grew alongside Wilfred. He would fuss and hum a lot, and we didn't know why. Yet when I sang to him, often lullabies from back home, he calmed. Once, I remember, we were coming back from Aldeburgh Food Festival in a car, and he was varying screams with drone-like hums. The music coming from our playlist wasn't working, but as soon as I opened my mouth he became quiet. I sang for three hours straight, red-faced and husky by the end, but it was worth it.

When our garden bloomed the following summer, I made sure to sing for him in the garden. He loved munching on the dill and the sorrel, and he still loved my singing, especially Ukrainian and Irish folk songs. I realised singing was good for my mental health too. I joined a choir called the Wing Its a month before the war began, because I suddenly felt an overwhelming urge to take my singing further. There we learned Ukrainian and Georgian polyphonic songs, which was what my heart was craving. When the conflict started we sang multiple Ukrainian pieces in harmony and in solidarity, and it saved me. During those early-war choir sessions, I may have scream-sung, just as I did during Wilfred's birth (for this I am sorry, dear Wing Its), but in the face of so much death and suffering, that scream-song felt life-giving and cathartic.

I had to stop the choir, because life and war became too much, but I still sing to Wilf and I still sing in the garden.

As Bertolt Brecht said, 'In the dark times, will there also be singing? Yes, there will also be singing. About the dark times.' And I know too that there will be growing, of plants and children, life and light.

OF CIRCULAR TIME
AND VEGETABLES

David Keenan and Heather Leigh

DK: So, what would you say you've learned from having an allotment?

HL: I would say, patterns of life and death, the process, the acceptance that everything that lives in the garden dies in the garden and then lives in the garden again.

DK: And there are so many lifespans; there are perennials, annuals . . .

HL: There's ephemerals, there's bi-annuals . . .

DK: What do you think of all the plants that can only come back from seed; is there still a continuity there?

HL: Yes, because I think it's the same process. There might be a difference in lifespan but that's another important thing actually, because even the annuals, they live a year, if that.

DK: Like a butterfly, almost.

HL: And their purpose in their life is no more diminished than a tree that lives for years.

DK: A flower that blooms once is a flower that has bloomed, forever.

HL: Exactly, and you also learn that with the animals as well. I love that it really does feel like a microcosm, everything is in the garden, everything takes place in the garden.

DK: Everything. One of my favourite moments, certainly of the last year, was when this duck flew in and sat in the exact little corner where the sun was still shining, the sun was going down, but it found this little corner of sun left, it flew in and was just sitting there, basking in it. For a while it and its mate were living in a submerged bath in the allotment behind us.

HL: Ha ha.

DK: There is something beautiful in how that duck and us found that same paradisical moment together.

HL: How many times have I sat in that sunny spot at the end of the day to get the last of the sun? One of my greatest joys of last year in the garden, which was really one of our best years, our tenth year there . . .

DK: Why would you say it was one of our best years?

HL: Well, in terms of what we grew, absolutely, but the wildlife was spectacular and it's the first time that I've actually seen, and in this case they were great tits, tits that were born in our garden. They took a nesting box there, grew and then hung about our garden and our birdbath.

DK: How far does your territory stretch? For us, our allotment is a couple of miles away from our house.

HL: And it has everything I need.

DK: It feels like an extension of our own place.

DK: One of the things I've learned from having an allotment is that whatever you need is right there in front of you.

HL: Yeah.

DK: If you can only re-imagine it, rethink it, realise the gift of it. One of the big things about us is that we try not to spend much money on the allotment, which I think is an allotment ethos in a way.

HL: Yeah.

DK: Try and see what is there around you. Always, we've got recycled wood, and stuff like this. Every time I think of a project I want to do, I realise I have something already there, in the garden, that I can use for that, that I can transform into that.

HL: Yeah, it's even, it's beyond recycling in a way, recycling at home, you have your plastic and your glass and your paper separate to recycle, but it's different to actually, truly, making use, making re-use, of what's around you as what you need. One thing I'd like to do more this year is collecting our own seeds and propagating from our own seeds.

DK: Because again you have to be very specific as to what works on your own patch, what thrives, what doesn't, this plot is now over ten years old and we're finally starting to understand what does well, what doesn't, what beds work best for what, I love the subtlety and the gradations of that, there are even beds in your own plot that have different characteristics and attributes. It's like cooking in a way, understanding how your cooker works, how different pots work, parts of the oven.

HL: And it's fascinating that even though there are all these plots around us, they are all dramatically different. From one to the next.

DK: In what they can do, in what they can grow.

HL: Let's be honest, in our allotment we're probably one of the most committed to the whole lifestyle of the allotment; we're not just there to grow some veg or just hang out. It's like we're in Bolinas there, that's how it feels, sometimes.

DK: It reminds me of being in Calderbank at my grandfather's old allotment, it's a very old-school working-class thing, allotments, and I remember going to his allotment with him when I was a kid and the variety of people you would see there, some absolute madmen, some dangerous characters, nice guys, it feels like our allotment is like that too.

HL: Outlaw.

DK: Yes, outlaw, and you gotta figure out how to get along with everyone.

HL: That's a huge difference coming from the States. I grew up in Texas, so I don't remember any allotments at all. I know they exist in the bigger cities like New York City, but everyone has enough land on their property in Texas that they can garden on that if they wanna garden, there's not that kind of specific allotment.

DK: And yet most people in Texas don't.

HL: Ha ha, depends, yeah.

DK: I almost feel as if in a Texas suburb a vegetable garden would kind of be rude or be seen as messy or something.

HL: And I think there is something to be said for your garden being separate from your living space. It's a different thing.

DK: Why?

HL: Well, I even wonder if we tended a garden in the back of our flat if it would really be the same vibe, even in terms of having a hut and a structure, that's one thing, but just the vibe of the allotment and that mix of people versus, well, we have our private space there, but it's never completely private, never can be. And yet you give so much to it and you don't own it and you will never own it.

DK: Well, that ends up going back to the whole Gary Snyder thing where you look at where you are, at the specifics of what you have to work with, and you look after your particular plot of earth in the way you can. See where you are and what you can do there. For no reason, actually, for no reason maybe except tenderness, except for maternal and paternal instincts that tending your appointed piece of land brings out. There's something beautiful about having a little plot on the earth that you are responsible for. And you want to make it beautiful.

HL: Yeah, you feel, you do feel you are a guardian.

DK: And it pays you back. I mean, when I was growing up I did not come from a household that you would call cultured, in terms of food culture, art, anything really, and so a lot of these things I hadn't even tasted. I'm thinking of my favourite things that I have discovered by growing them in our allotment and I would have to say broad beans. Broad beans have been a revelation to me. And also because of the little window you realise they exist in, every year for me, podding them, the whole ritual of it, of bringing them up indoors, of planting them out, making sure they are okay, some of them getting savaged by rodents and deer. The ones that make it through. And then that first ritual of podding the broad beans. Put some music on, pour a glass of wine. It's such a beautiful ritual. And the taste and the flavour. I think that sort of tying up of time, of circular time and vegetables, is beautiful, something really expressive about that, of what is.

HL: I feel a similar ritual with gathering cut flowers from the garden and arranging bouquets and getting lost in that project.

DK: Well, it's interesting that flowers aren't a big part of allotments and in fact are discouraged, in a way, but we've really

come to balance our vegetable growing with our flower growing, and the flower growing was a later development.

HL: At first we were maybe a bit focused just on the veg,
because there was the challenge of the new plot, figuring out
what you could even grow. And it being not of the highest
quality when we got it, us being responsible for working with
it to get it to where it's at now, where it is so fertile. That was
the priority, at first.

DK: Yeah, in terms of fertility, you talked earlier on about the
miracle that life grows out of death, that vegetables grow
out of decomposed matter, dead materials, and that's definitely one of the big revelations, and one of the biggest ones
for me – which a lot of people are coming to, and you know
more about this than I do – is the whole concept of 'no dig',
leaving the soil as it is. To me that is so miraculous and
beautiful, that you really don't need to do anything for the
earth to provide your food.

HL: You don't.

DK: That is, like, wild. Why are we paying for shit? Know
what I mean?

HL: Yeah, I mean in ideal conditions, and even in unideal
conditions, actually, sometimes the more unideal conditions
the better, where the roots really have to work, where the

plants have to work a bit to survive and if you leave the soil and all the organisms and all the fungi to do its work, it will do its work.

DK: I remember one summer when this massive ant colony moved into one of our compost bins and at first I was freaked out, if you took the lid off they would all start running mad, acting crazy, but we just left it and at the end of that year they moved out and left us with the best compost we have ever had, it was so fine and soft and pure and just smelled great. So crumbly, beautiful. You kind of feel you're involved in this thing where you are collaborating with these wee beasts.

HL: It is a collaboration.

DK: What's your favourite stuff you have grown in the garden?

HL: I love all the flowers, hellebore, the rudbeckias, the heleniums, I love when a poppy appears, the fritillary, snake's head fritillary in particular, roses. I'd like to try cucumbers again, the wee cucumbers; I love their curly tendrils, they are so beautiful. Tomatoes are always a joy and that was such a great thing this year that has never happened before where, well, birds have broken into our greenhouse and our hut before, but never have I caught a blue tit decimating cherry tomatoes on the vine with a friend, or a sibling, who knows. And that was one of the most joyous things. And I should say, I do very much love to document our allotment, I love taking photographs. Making books of those photographs and somehow understanding the space that way too.

DK: One of the things that had a massive effect this year was bringing more water into the garden. We redid our pond and we also put a bird bath in, how revolutionary was that?

HL: Yeah. The effect was amazing.

DK: It's like the smallest little gesture can be completely transformative. Maximum payback. The bird situation was insane because of that. And also beasts in the pond. Is there anything more beautiful than a bird bathing?

HL: Yes, with luck we will get some newts this year, and dragonflies, which we did see. A damselfly, this year, actually, for the first time in the garden. And I could watch birds bathe all day long, to be honest, I could, absolutely gorgeous.

DK: We should say that our allotment is not like a normal allotment. It's pretty wild.

HL: No, if you walk around our allotment, it's quite clear, I don't see, well, certainly in terms of wildlife, although there is a bee keeper around that we haven't met yet, but outside of that I don't see much evidence that people have much concern for the birds or wildlife.

DK: And often not much concern about their garden . . . ha
ha . . . but what I like about our allotment is that it is a
little feral, and over the years, I wish we had documented
it, although you have been good at taking photographs,
there's classic little huts and beautiful gardens that are now
long destroyed, gone for more than a decade now, but I can
recall so many of them, that were so gorgeous, you know. I
think it's a working-class thing, I can imagine my dad doing
it himself, where when you take over a garden it's like a
scorched-earth policy; you destroy everything in it and then
start from scratch. But a lot of these guys move in, destroy
everything, and then never come back. Sometimes I think
I have almost imagined some of these huts that I believe I
have visited, some of the strange characters I have had teas
with in gloomy wooden huts hidden away in corners of the
allotment. I remember huts built up on stilts at the bottom
of the allotment, in the shadow of the tall trees, with guys
trying to build huts as high on stilts as they could to get to
the sunlight, sitting with these guys in complete darkness
and having a cup of tea with them in their weird hut. I know
it existed in one way, that I was there, once, but was I really?
There are parts of the allotment that I have never revisited
because I don't even want to know if it was true or not or if it
has transformed in my memory. It also goes back to a lifelong
obsession with huts and with hutting, you know, *Woodstock*

Handmade Houses, all this kind of stuff, I can't think of anything more beautiful than a handmade wooden home.

HL: Well, it goes back to our first hut, which we bought in Carbeth, just outside Glasgow.

DK: Yes, and we lived there for a bit.

HL: What was interesting about that was it was really about the hut. We didn't garden there at all, really, we just focused on hutting, and that's what I mean perhaps even about how there is something special about the allotment itself. We didn't make an effort to get a veg patch or even flowers going at the hut, with time we would have perhaps, versus the allotment, where you just dive into it right away.

DK: Or was it that we were older when we got an allotment? If we got a hut now of course we would dig a vegetable plot. I guess what you are saying is that with an allotment you are specifically there to grow. Although I would have to say, most of the people on our allotment are not there to grow.

HL: Well, there's a few exemplars, however, that are so focused on the growing it's not necessarily about any garden aesthetic; they are just there to grow.

DK: Well, in a way I understand that people want plots there because they want to live wild; they want to sit and watch a fire there, at night. It's almost like they want to regress. I totally understand that. It is an ethos that is deep inside me. There is a part of me that would love to rip out the central heating from our flat and survive with open fires burning bits of wood that we scavenge from the garden.

HL: Yeah, totally.

DK: Surviving off your own wits, the daily routine of carrying water and chopping wood, is more fun, is more satisfying.

HL: There is something so satisfying about working with the earth, feeling the pull of a weed from the soil.

DK: That little pop of resistance.

HL: And revealing an earthworm. Watching it work.

DK: We often talk about how garden work is like meditation, because you are so in the zone; there is no room for thoughts when you are plucking weeds. Or like nipping out the side-shoots from a tomato plant and smelling it on your fingers.

HL: I'd go so far as to say that I am probably more in a true meditative state when I am gardening than when I sit for meditation. I feel my mind perhaps is a bit more silent when I'm in the garden or maybe I'm just not paying attention to the mind.

DK: I guess in meditation you are more watching the mind, whereas when you are gardening you're truly out of your mind.

HL: And you always are reaping the rewards of your work, even a very simple bit of weeding or watering, putting something new in a container, all of these things have an immediate satisfaction to them. Though there's the opposite too; it's a place of opposites, joining. I mean some things you really have to wait to get them to flower. Or to see them establish themselves. Sometimes you get excited and it seems like it is establishing, and then it dies. And you can't be attached. You just plant something else. It is a constant learning process in that way, I don't think you can ever stop learning in the garden and there are no guaranteed results. Because one year something can do super well and the next year it can completely fail and you swore you hadn't changed any of the conditions. But that's just the way it goes.

DK: And it can break your heart. So much of our sweet peas were devoured last year. Every time I went up my heart was in my throat to see how they were doing. One was coming through and starting to climb up a little rope and it felt so wonderful, against all the odds, it had made it through. You were semi-devoured, you had two of your leaves bit off, and look at you climbing that rope . . . unassuaged.

HL: Such joy in the little things.

DK: I think when we remade our pond this year, it really came back to me how entranced I was by pond life when I was a kid. A big thing for us was searching out ponds on the outskirts of Airdrie. Skaters, minnows, frogs, toads . . . sometimes when I stare at that pond and I see the little water boatmen rising to the surface or scurrying back to the depths, it is like staring into time, that it is the same little body of water come back to me that fascinated me first when I was eleven. It really does reconcile you to what Joseph Campbell says, that life feeds on life, that death is the cost of life, death is fertile with life, which if you've only ever bought a spud from Tesco it might be an idea, but not a lived reality.

UNCERTAIN GROUND

Marchelle Farrell

The allotment is not what I expected. There are no neat rows of plots, some with small sheds or twee seating areas at the end. There is no committee, no signs up declaring the site's rules or advertising upcoming community events. There is simply a padlocked gate onto a field, as anonymous as any other privately demarcated plot of land in the surrounding countryside patchwork. We go through the gate from the village car park on a dull, early spring morning, having been granted the code for the lock. A thrill to be let into this secret space. We walk down the lightly trodden path through late winter-brown, knee-high grass, past curious chickens in an enclosure under just-leafing trees next to a full-height vegetable cage full of purple sprouting broccoli. The plot that is to be partly ours is at the end, an empty pig shed in the space beyond it. A rickety fence surrounds the whole area. An overgrown hedge, still largely bare of leaves, lies at the back of the plot, which seems to be mostly made up of bits of old carpet and tarpaulin in between a sea of nettles.

We go through the listing gate and stand uncertainly, looking at the space. I tread down a couple of nettles and scuff up some earth with the toe of my wellies. Stooping, I pick up a handful of soil; it is dark brown and crumbles between my fingers, a reassuringly rich loam. I brush off my hands and turn away from the flat, weedy patch we have inherited to look at the valley falling away from it to the brook out of sight and earshot below, and then rising again beyond. With loam-stained fingers, I shade my eyes as I squint up at the overcast sky. Apart from a strip sheltered by the hedge rapidly turning into trees at the back, this plot is in full sun, with well-draining soil, the opposite of our steeply shaded, heavy-clay, moist garden. The children promptly climb into an old bath discarded against the fence and begin to play a high-stakes game that involves sailing through a sea of nettles without getting stung. My husband and I look at each other, pick up our tools and set to work.

I never intended to have an allotment. They were not a thing to desire where I grew up. In the urban sprawl occupying a densely creeping band across the north-east of Trinidad, hemmed in on three sides by mountains, marsh-land and the sea, there seemed little thought of growing spaces, little call for them. There were parks in the older town centres, vestiges of colonial city-planning given the names of dead governors or queens. For most of my childhood we lived near the largest grouping of urban green space, within walking distance of the Queen's Park Savannah, the Royal Botanic Garden, the Hollows and Memorial Square. These parks were composed of tamed trees, closely clipped lawn, disused fountains and impeccably tended planting, neat white stripes painted around the bottom of palm trees. They were spaces that had been reclaimed from the colonial landlords when they were ousted, for public leisure and enjoyment, but the legacy of their creation lingered and their planting was heavily controlled and policed. For people to come together over a plot of land in these public areas in the shared act of growing for nourishment was unthinkable. In the weeding out of that story of relating to land, we had lost our common ground.

In the suburban gardens of my earliest childhood, much of the growing was either ornamental or fruit trees. My grandmother spent a great deal of time gardening, focused on tending her beloved roses and other decorative plants in her proud front garden, while setting her teenage sons the task of managing the mango, avocado and citrus of various sorts in the back yard. Other than the fruit, her only concession to growing plants for consumption was an aloe vera by the kitchen door and a few other herbs used for their medicinal properties. Often made to drink the bitter aloe's water – for the cooling she thought that my fiery temperament needed – I held no appreciation for these plants. In our neighbourhood, perhaps the odd person raised their own patch of pigeon peas, or harvested sorrel for Christmas, but most of the veg we ate came from the local shop or the market, much of it imported from other Caribbean islands or further overseas. I had a few friends who lived more rurally or owned land out in 'de bush', as we named the tropical rainforest wilderness on the hills. But their relationship with that land seemed mostly to involve hunting local wild meat to be feasted on for parties and for pleasure.

There was some agricultural activity on the island still, though mostly the economy relied on oil and gas drilled and pumped from fields offshore. When I was very young, cows roamed the expanse of grass we called the savannah, which lay at the end of the cul-de-sac my grandparents lived on, though they had disappeared by the time I was a teen. The goats that grazed verges on less busy roads, or the yard fowl once commonly kept for their eggs and the Sunday roast, similarly faded from view. Farmers grew food at scale, and we needed them, and yet there was an unspoken snobbery about their necessary work. They did not sit high up in the island's inherited hierarchy of social class. To live off the land in that way was somehow dirty, and marked you as poor. To return to working the earth as many of our ancestors had been forcibly brought to the island to do was a backwards step in our progression away from the shackles of history. I strode forward into the white sterility of medical training to my community's great joy and blessings.

The word 'allotment' had no meaning in my Caribbean childhood. Or none that anyone I knew wanted to reclaim. The only allotments that I encountered were in history books, the tiny allocations of land on plantations that enslaved people tended in their limited spare time in order to try to grow small crops of food and medicine for themselves. What food? Which medicines? Our history books skipped over these superfluous facts. Did they grow black-eyed peas? Originating in West Africa, did those dried beans with the central black spot that presumably gave them their name come with the people on the slave ships to these Caribbean islands, along with the traditional belief that they must be eaten on New Year's Day for prosperity and good luck? I try to imagine the scene, holding on to a belief in prosperity and good luck when so much else had been savagely stolen. Did the small patch of earth that they tended hold on to that faith in something better? Did they imagine a patch of land to tend freely one day?

*

It is hard to know where to start with this unruly parcel of land. We are sharing it with another villager, given the offer of the space after her previous allotment partner moved away. Her side has been tended, and looks recognisably like the outlines of a vegetable garden waiting for the growth of spring, but ours looks as though it has been neglected for quite some time.

We begin by peeling up the disintegrating membranes, tarpaulins and mats that had once been laid in an effort to suppress the plants now gleefully entangled among them. My husband hoes up swathes of bright-green, spring-fresh nettles while I follow him slowly, squatting and picking over the residues of plastic and ropes of bindweed in the soil. After a couple of hours my lower back feels as knotted as the bucketsful of white roots I have been pulling from the soil. Stretching, I stand and look around at what we have managed to clear and prepare for planting. I am dismayed; it does not look like very much. But my husband is cheerfully optimistic, pleased with the space. He slings his tools over his shoulder and whistles as he sets off along the path back to the car park. The children race up from the field and follow after. I linger a moment, to cast one last worried look at this extra project we have taken on. This greedy surplus of land when so few have any. As I look, I realise that sunlight has burned through the overcast skies as we worked, and is now sparkling on the buds and just-unfurling leaves of the hedge at the back. I can hear the fervent nesting song of birds hidden among the branches. As I turn to leave, I pick a small bouquet of nettle tops to be steeped in a pot of tea back at home, in the superstitious hope that the plants might somehow tell me how it will be in their space.

At least all the nettles reassure us that the soil of the plot is fertile. We decide to attempt potatoes, planting rows and rows of them in the growing patch of earth that we partially reclaim from the bindweed and nettles. We are reading Joy Larkcom's guide to vegetable growing in the lengthening evenings, and she recommends potatoes as a good initial crop to break in neglected soil and suppress other, less desired plants. The suggestion delights my husband and daughter, both fond of a starchy tuber, and three kilo bags of blue, purple and red heritage seed potato varieties arrive in the post, and then jostle for space to chit in the front porch. It takes us days to plant them all.

When we first arrived in our new house in the countryside, taking on an allotment was the furthest thing from my mind. We suddenly had over a third of an acre of garden where we had had none before. Coming to terms with the land we now had under our care felt urgent and overwhelming enough;

I couldn't imagine seeking more. We gratefully threw ourselves into the space when a pandemic locked us within it, amateurishly sowing seeds along with what seemed to be the entire nation. We planted our uncertain seedlings into the garden's old, precarious veg beds and tended them as they grew. Later we harvested from the survivors until the beds rotted away and fell down the hillside and grew too unsafe to use. That autumn, we built new veg beds on the small lawn, one of the only flat areas of our site. It was not ideal. Sitting as it did just behind the house meant that it was heavily shaded for most of the year, but it was a kitchen garden just outside our kitchen, where we imagined that we would look out of the windows and see our harvest.

Growing food turned out to be hard work. Our soil was heavy and wet. By contrast, the organic peat-free compost I had ordered to fill the no-dig beds we had created turned out to be disappointingly dusty and dry. Our garden lay in a frost pocket, so our soil was cold till late in the year, and trying to get our seedlings strong enough to thrive in it without a greenhouse was a trial. There was a healthy population of slugs, the vast majority of which seemed to congregate in the veg beds. There were hedgehogs and frogs, slow-worms and even glow-worm larvae too, but not enough to stem the tide of voracious slimy creatures decimating our lettuce. I thought about getting ducks, but felt ill-prepared for livestock if I couldn't keep even vegetables alive. I gave up on lettuce and tried chard, which the slugs seemed less interested in, but which tempted the deer out of the nearby woods. Bending over the beds with our struggling crops, I felt the full force of my resistance to food growing, and my resentment of it. To bend and labour over the earth triggered a pain in my psyche that was generations deep. One that I had been taught to turn away from, to concrete over, box in with reinforced glass and steel. I thrust my hands into the earth with seeds and seedlings anyway, resolved to gain some nourishment out of my burgeoning relationship with the soil. The peas that survived the mice eventually did well. Broad beans, garlic and brassicas too. A courgette turned into a monstrous marrow seemingly overnight. The children complained about how much of it there was to eat, but I was relieved to find that there were indeed some things we could grow. I thought it was all that we needed.

So, when one day at the school gates a neighbour asked if we would like to share her plot, my first instinct was to decline. I felt as though we were barely managing our own garden; to take on an allotment as well seemed madness. But my husband was keen. He thought it would offer us the growing conditions that we simply did not have in our own garden: less frost, warmer and drier soil, more sun. It would allow us to try a wider range of food with a better chance of a useful harvest. But more persuasive than this, my curiosity was piqued. I had heard that there were allotments in the village but knew they were not the traditionally operated, local council-run sort. I wanted to understand them, to find out what function they served in this place where I imagined that everyone had their own country garden. Intrigue got the better of me. I agreed to come take a look and see.

There turned out to be two small allotment sites in the village. Both privately owned parcels of land, loaned out to those neighbours whose homes were carved out of the erratically divided up former small farms in the centre of the village in such a way as to leave them with no garden to grow in. The allotment site at the top of the hill just above our house seemed to have no vacancies. And we were told that with our generous garden the owner and gatekeeper of the space would have been unlikely to deem us deserving of a place. We wandered in once when the gate was invitingly open as we walked past. There were no signs advising us to keep out, but the knowledge that this was really a neighbour's bit of land, despite the communal culture of allotments, made setting foot into the space feel illicit. A form of trespass. To one side of the otherwise neatly tended area was a rampant patch of raspberry plants dripping with fruit, some already rotting on the canes. We did not discourage the children from helping themselves to all they could eat. It seemed a shameful waste otherwise.

The other allotments in which we were to be granted our eventual patch lay on the opposite side of the village, further from our home. One strip of plots along the western edge of the field looked professionally tended – I had no doubt that some of the prize-winning specimens on display in the village's traditional annual flower show were grown here. I could imagine pencil-straight runner beans and neat, regulation courgettes in a few months' time. The strip to which our plot belonged along the northern edge of the field was wilder, and more unruly. The arrangement we entered to grow on the space was an informal one. A token amount of rent paid to the landowner annually, meant to cover water usage, though our plot had no tap, only the cracked bathtub commandeered by the children. A gift of extra space, benevolently bestowed by the landowner who seemed to like me, my keen interest in gardening, my desire to grow community and reconnection with the earth alongside my crops.

The field on which our allotment sat was held in joint ownership, with the party with whom we dealt holding the lion's share of its worth. The history of the space, pieced together from fragmentary conversations, seemed to tell a story of initial idealism that over time had transformed into something more jaded. It appeared that friends had once

unevenly clubbed together to buy this field and a neighbouring orchard. There was a nostalgic sense in the stories of a
vision of something more communal and collective, feeding
a community of neighbours from this shared land. Over the
years, it had seemingly not come to fruition. When I mis-
takenly announced a wassail for the orchard in the village
newsletter, an attempt at a fun way for people to gather and
to teach our children about the rites of the growing season in
traditional cider country, I was reminded that I had not sought
permission to advertise the event, and that information about
the gathering should be disseminated along private channels
to suit the status of the land. Chastened, I reread the friendly
and polite email and wondered where the line lay between
the cynicism that came with ownership and the care that
accompanied stewardship. I emailed my apology, withdrew
the public notice, and messaged on WhatsApp groups instead,
thinking all the while about the corrupting power of land's
monetary worth.

I supposed that if we were to fit any allotment, it would
be this unlikely one, carved from a weedy patch of land on
the scrappy edge of a field. A piece of land generously loaned,
but the precarious conditionality of which leaves me feeling
as though I am trying to root into uncertain ground. As a black
immigrant trying to make a home in the UK, I am always trying
to root into uncertain ground. But I wondered how different

it really was from the allotments we had walked past in the city we lived in before, where friends hoped for years on long waiting lists for the gift of a space. Where most of the plots lay in the more affluent areas of the city where the houses tended to have gardens anyway. And I wondered what connection any of this now held to the original allotments in the history books of my childhood, rooted as they were in a system of loaning out a patch of land to the labouring poor so that they might attempt to grow a bit to eat.

At summer's end we harvest our crop. We have been back since, planting our potatoes, weeding and earthing them up in snatched moments between the increasing pace of work and school as the world once again speeds up after its pandemic pause. They have done well, and we uncover generous piles of tubers. The children are delighted by the colours, running around exclaiming with wonder at red and blue versions of this vegetable they know so well in brown. We place them still muddy in trays as an attempt to store them over the coming months in the cool basement.

We take the chance to comb through the soil disturbed by uprooting the potatoes, removing as many bindweed roots as we can, then begin planting out alliums to fill some of the space over winter. They are less likely to compete well with the plot's established plants, but they are an easy 'set and forget'-style crop, needing minimal intervention until harvesting – provided that rain comes when it should. And I have begun dreaming of spring, of what crops we could try in this space next year. Dahlias maybe, which will not grow in my own damp, slug-endowed garden but might thrive in this sunny spot. I imagine their flowers but, if they do well enough, we could try them for the original purpose for which they were grown by the indigenous people of Central America, not far from the country of my birth. We could eat the tubers as well. And to make this plot of land with its uncertain relationship between the private and the communal feel more like home ground, I have ordered some seeds.

I have not found black-eyed peas that might thrive here, but a type of northern-adapted pigeon pea that should crop within our shorter growing season. Pigeon peas travelled like black-eyed peas from the West African lands of their origin to the Caribbean. Eaten year-round using tinned peas in a traditional rice-based dish called pelau, fresh bags of pigeon peas were in season at the end of the year to appear stewed on a laden Christmas table, the ultimate expression of the year's prosperity and good luck. I think of the packets of dried-out, dull-green seeds as I prepare the soil. What will it feel like to grow a crop so connected with my childhood? To gain the comfort of familiar nourishment from this different land?

What would it feel like to grow on true common ground? Owned by no one but the land itself, what would it mean to grow free? There is perhaps no real knowing on this private patch of ground, but I will sow my seeds into the earth and see.

LAND IS THE WORK
OF MANY HANDS

Jenny Chamarette

Outside his final house, he worships life.
Jenny Mitchell, 'A Man in Love with Plants'*

The site is well concealed, hidden by houses on three sides. On the fourth a park, along whose top corner trundles a rutted private road, threaded with nettles. The wooden gates are high and gunmetal grey (once pale green before the graffiti) and padlocked with a shared key. From there you pass through a short, narrowish passageway between two fenced-off gardens. A camellia bush to your right, next to a tender vine that weeps green-gold in late autumn; in winter ground elder and aconites shift across the beaten earth. To your left, steps

---

* From *Resurrection of a Black Man* (Indigo Dreams Publishing, 2022).

up to the wooden cabin that houses the composting toilet. An ash tree in late-stage dieback, and several taller, healthier sycamores frame the entrance to open ground.

When my partner and I arrived at our allotment for the first time in the warm, weak skies of October 2019, we came through this portal framed by trees. For four, nearly five years, alone and with others, I have witnessed its threshold, a small grid reference placed on a map of space and time. I've photographed it often: each moment takes on different colours, flavours, moods. Each one holds the grace of its arrival, and the grief of its passing.

The allotment is mine only to hold, never to own. And it frames me too. It shapes me in ways I am learning to express. Access to land – and by access I mean neither property nor ownership – is fundamental to how all of us come to know ourselves. I am no different.

It's a small thing, a plot – and yet also not. The traditional allocation is ten rods, each rod equivalent to a 5.5 × 5.5-yard square. Ours is technically a half: five rods, an area of around 126 square metres. Once you subtract the paths between beds, the box container for tools and gardening supplements inherited from a previous plot holder, the compost heap, and the pile of rubble and earth left unturned for a season or two, there is less growing space. Still far more land than I can conceive of owning in my lifetime.

I often compare its size to the considerably smaller footprint of our one-bedroom flat. Property has no footprints in a literal sense; only the carbon effects of cumulative construction. Sometimes I fantasise about planting my feet here instead, between the plot, communal toilet and community shed. Of course this whimsy is rudely interrupted by winter's realities: no heating, electricity, or even running water when the mains supply is switched off to protect underground pipes from bursting.

On our small parcel of land there are no walls, only beds for growing. Some have semi-permanent residents: rhubarb, gooseberries, black and white currants, raspberries, strawberries, gladioli, a hot-pink rose, lavender, two clematis (one lilac, one white). Others are briefer bedfellows who change with the seasons and the years. My few dalliances with sweetcorn, for example, have left me dissatisfied. I never grow them sweet or full enough. Both qualities are perspectival, anyway: ants dive into their frothy ends, leaving the tips gnawed bare.

We operate an inefficient form of crop rotation, which generally involves not planting the same thing in the same place, year on year. Most of the time we are pushed for space, and the mapping of crop rotation to vegetable bed blurs around the edges. Our harvests are mutable and movable. And though they seem irrational, they are in fact meticulously tied to time in the ground, daylight hours, microbiome, soil and air temperature, nutrient levels, soil density, humidity, disease, memory, determination. It is not the fault of our crops that they know more than me about the land. I fall in and out of love with them as they grow, wither and succumb, or alternatively flourish into a glut that first excites and then overwhelms.

This November there is celery wrapped in cardboard and twine to blanch it. Pairs of celeriac grow bulbous, crowns lifted above the soil. Frayed strings of early leeks languish in the mud; rows of land cress, winter lettuces, tatsoi and mizuna fight cheerfully; kale frills and primps its early shoots, Brussels sprouts bud quietly towards a midwinter harvest. Not all beds are full: we recently took down overgrown pumpkins from their vertical frames. The ground below is strewn with shrivelled leaves and skeins of tomato roots pulled in October.

Our five-rod growing space lurches between industrious labour and temporary shambles. With each season I learn a little more about my mistakes and naiveties. The plot responds erratically and with unnerving regularity. This year's ragged leeks mostly vanished with the early slug onslaught. Purple tatsoi are laced with a million tiny holes, courtesy of flea beetles. The shallow-bottomed celeriac have trailing root nests that are difficult to scrub clean for cooking. Bushels of celery are crowded with woodlice, who I gently discourage when I harvest the hearts. Perhaps if I'd pulled them sooner, if we'd blanched earlier, we'd have fewer terrestrial crustaceans. But I am not sure that would be a good thing.

A thick tangle of brambles runs along one edge of the plot. When clearing its edges earlier this year I noticed the decaying food trails of mice. Dropped roots, remnants of burst tomatoes and berry seeds led tiny paths through the thicket. Sometimes saying the obvious out loud is important. The plot was and is never ours exclusively.

The minor and inconsequential discoveries of our tenure beget strange companionship; small, intimate feelings. More than food or space, the plot breeds quietude. Acceptance of the botch, the flop, the fiasco. And also something focused and fascinated and diligent: not quite sexual, but a little like it. I would be lying if I said that there wasn't some small erotic charge in the repetition of growth, glut and ruin, and my insistent attention to all three. There's a feeling, generative and edgy, beyond what words can usefully express.

Here is what I know from knowing my plot. Food growing on an allotment is an act of mutual consent between humans, plants, climate and an unimaginably extensive range of soil-based life forms. In relationship to land I learn how I am always connected, even when I fumble. The land does not abandon me when I am inadequate to the task of caring for it. When I don't have the language to describe these intimate, queer – yes, queer – feelings of land. Sexuality, love, joy, grief. Failure too, though that comes later.

There is wisdom in knowing land, in loving it. And it is a crime that this intimacy of land-knowing, land-loving, is not available to all. The most longstanding and brutal forms of human cruelty have all involved dispossession from land. Colonisation, occupation, enclosure, extraction and exploitation, war and its ecological devastations, mass pollution, land clearances and over-cultivation, forced migration, urbanisation: all sever people and beings from their roots in the land – or in the case of nomadic cultures, in the landscape, the weather, the earth's spirit.

If intimacy with land were simple, then, as we hurtle towards our own destruction through biodiversity loss and climate crisis, exponential wealth inequality and chronic food insecurity, we humans wouldn't feel so divided. Land disconnection is a first-world problem for sure, since colonial nations created it in the first place. Over the last four hundred years it has spread certainly and irrevocably across the globe, as successive waves of colonial power terminally disrupted countless indigenous land relationships, and then their own back home. I feel it too on the allotment, the pull of disconnection. I can't pretend I don't. But I am also learning, relearning, something much older than me.

Don't misunderstand me: I still live a long way from ecological truth. Various unspoken powers uphold my land-growing and land-knowing. For example: the lease of an allotment is preceded by a number of small but crucial underlying elements. You have to know you will be living in one place for an extended period of time. The intention needs to be there, but also the possibility. This necessitates some degree of social and domestic security. The financial indemnity to maintain your home arrangements. In other words, you need to feel and be safe enough to persist, to remain. If I say that safety has been hard enough for me to come by, with all the structural advantages I have been afforded, what I mean to say is: it is not a guarantee. It takes a long time to forge a relationship with the land. Sometimes it doesn't happen at all. Staying power is the power to stay. Only some of that is self-willed.

I also mean to say: land intimacy is a fundamental right, a fundamental responsibility. The confiscation and annexation of land divorces people from their most intimate relationship with earth. Land is neither to be owned nor requisitioned. It is to be grown. It is to be known, with many hands.

I sit at the earliest end of what has been described as the millennial generation, straddled between the lower birth rates and higher living standards associated with Gen X, and the entrepreneurial, community-oriented Gen Z. These designations don't mean much. Cultural currencies that like to circulate from time to time, trying and failing to create tribes and separations. I'm suspicious of their white, Euro-Western tang: the flavour of the specific masquerading as the universal. Still, by dint of being born in the UK in the early 1980s and with sufficient cultural capital to go to university, my student loan was not a lifetime's yoke. I also made the error of coming into existence too late to receive a university education with a maintenance grant and no fees. I lived through the traumatic effects of Section 28, the legislation that prohibited any discussion of homosexuality in publicly funded schools. And yet, alongside the shady aftermath of sequential post-colonial wars in the Middle East and elsewhere, I witnessed the socio-economic shifts in early 2000s Britain and Europe that facilitated wider social cohesion, for some, including me. Providence built my tender adolescent identity as European; government then stole it away. Joy is often crisscrossed with privilege, and the allotment is both.

In the waning sun of October 2019, my partner and I reaped the harvest of our situational good fortune, and chose a sunny, overgrown plot, close to the central path that runs south–north towards the communal sheds. On our first day, we cut back brambles and sifted the accumulated rubble, rocks, plastic, wood, ceramics, canes, bricks and old tools. It was satisfying, geometric work, clearing this smallish rectangle of its largest objects. I do not come from an agricultural family, and am generally unused to spending time with the land. I am in the process of learning, later but not too late, what *land use* means. How the land has oral histories passed down between the people who tend it, and what they leave behind.

As we sit on garden chairs by the communal shed in summer 2020, eating roasted squashes and clean, tight, red tomatoes, a fellow plot holder tells me that there were once greenhouses here. I have never seen them, not even a photograph. I wouldn't know where to find one. Still, my dreams unearth long white-framed corridors of glass, spooling out cucumbers, vines, melons, peaches, all scrubbed clean of marauding insects. Every pastoral idyll carries its counterweight: the Victorians, like their British forebears and descendants were masterful in the extermination of more-than-human species. In early twentieth-century horticultural journals, the total obliteration of pests and wildlife is mentioned with pride. Albeit that Fiona Davison's recent biography of six early twentieth-century women gardeners* is about the radical gardening paths forged by white middle- and upper-class women, their letters to one another are littered with death-sentiment. Pests are the enemy, to be removed at all costs.

I'm not wholly judging this lust for killing. When other, smaller creatures threaten your food security, the desire to exterminate is often activated. But the cultivation of tender fruit is hard to square with the mass destruction of invertebrates. The desire to foster a haven of safety is often

---

* Fiona Davison, *An Almost Impossible Thing: The Radical Lives of Britain's Pioneering Women Gardeners* (Little Toller, 2023).

inseparable from the desire to eradicate the other lives who infiltrate it. Death is not the answer to utopia. And yet . . .

And yet I see it still, this killing-lust, in wars unfolding right now, when ecological devastation is wrought on land and people. What is written small in the land is also writ large in the world.

Before the hothouses and cold frames were smashed to pieces by the bombing raids of the Second World War, produce grown here likely fed the wealthy landowners of the inner city. Perhaps too the affluent Victorian commuters, whose recently purchased country homes built on the steep crest of London's southern borders were just a short train ride away from London Bridge. It's possible, but perhaps a little less likely, that cucumbers and peaches also fed a few members of the village that is now my home. Until 1889 this village was part of the Kentish countryside: its transformation into *London* came about as a result of local government electoral reforms in 1888.

From my allotment it is a short, steep walk to the top of the Norwood Ridge that once flanked the southern limits of the nineteenth-century city. The rise – the highest till you reach the North Downs – now overlooks the sweep of contemporary London. From here you come eye to eye with the glittering shards of Canary Wharf, Southwark and the City.

Distance is deceptive: on clear days ambient distributions of light bring them close. Standing on the crest, I scan the contents of this wide bowl scooped from millions of years of sediment. I'm reminded of the deep geological time over which London is thinly spread. This is one of the pleasures of land, seeing what lies beneath the cultural strata. I don't hate this city. But when tidelines of air pollution regularly choke the high-rises, and blue sky fades to tawny haze, it leaves its mark.

Leeward of the geological summit whose clay beds were once brick kilns for Victorian and Edwardian housing, there was, more than likely, a market garden where the allotment now sits. Historically the market gardens of London were to the south-west, where richer land was supplemented by the euphemistically described *night soil* of Londoners. But then, just as now, there was room to grow on the claggy terrain of south-east London's rises and plateaus. In any case, those greenhouses were destroyed, and the land became a bomb site and a trash heap. Many allotments were started on contaminated ground: this isn't unusual. A 2019 study even made the case that edible plants grown on allotments could provide useful data about ambient levels of air pollution.[*] Plants are incredible phytoremediators. Sunflowers (*Helianthus annuus L.*) and Indian

---

[*] Miguel Izquierdo-Díaz et al., 'Urban Allotment Gardens for the Biomonitoring of Atmospheric Trace Element Pollution', *Journal of Environmental Quality*, vol. 48 no. 2 (March–April 2019), pp. 518–25.

mustard (*Brassica juncea L.*) both process industrial waste and heavy metals from the soil, transforming land into a safer environment for other beings, human and otherwise.

Under an awning in patches between rain clouds, another allotmenteer tells me that railway carriages were stored here, after the glasshouses were lost. In 1965 sweeping closures of the rail networks took place, instigated by then chairman of British Railways Baron Richard Beeching. Both the person and his programme were thereafter known as the Beeching Axe, which left plentiful trains in the wake of its destruction. I hear it said that carriages were sold for £5 each, with £1 for delivery.

Like the glasshouses before them, there are no wagons here now. Though sometimes I hear their electric descendants saluting from half a mile away, along the line that runs southwards towards the Kent countryside.

Owning an allotment is cheap in some ways. The land is never owned by the individuals who work it. It is rented for a small sum of money per year, usually from voluntary societies who run the allotment on behalf of local government councils, or charities, or private corporations. Nonetheless, waiting lists are long: our three years was small fry in London, where demand for land for urban agriculture heavily outstrips supply. This might go some way to explaining why allotments are often seen as the preserve of the white middle classes seeking the 'Good Life', those who have the material resources of wealth and leisure to be able to turn a grassy, bramble-and-trash-filled patch into a thriving plot. Even so, the demographics of our allotment are neither particularly white, nor British, nor middle-class. There is plenty of diversity if you stay long enough to notice. But the association between wealth, whiteness and land remains. Why wouldn't it? Long-term rental properties are on the wane as the predominantly unregulated private market has exploded. In the last twenty years land values in London have risen exponentially; a chronic shortage of affordable housing is the result of decades of land sell-off. None of this is news to anyone who lives in the south-east of England, or indeed most of the UK. In the Office for National Statistics' English Housing Survey 2023, 3.4 million homes – approximately 15 per cent of dwellings in England – failed to meet the Decent Homes Standard, the highest proportion of which were privately rented properties.[*] Stable, comfortable, secure housing, chosen at will, should be a minimum standard of living for all. And yet, it isn't.

Access to land for growing should be as simple as a name on a list. But in a capital-driven society, under a government uninterested in making life bearable for those who cannot

---

[*] English Housing Survey 2022 to 2023: headline report, 14 December 2023, https://www.gov.uk/government/collections/english-housing-survey-2022-to-2023-headline-report.

afford property, land ownership trumps land connection. House first; then you can wait for this plot, which is not yours.

I have spent countless hours with my hands in the claggy soil of this allotment. Gloved or ungloved, in brief interludes between midwinter downpours (and sometimes caught in the middle of them), in unexpected late frosts, at the height of dusty summers, I have become intimately acquainted with its dense, fine particulate matter. I have felt mud settle into my pores, held worms and centipedes in my palm as I pull them away from the tines of my fork while turning over a freshly manured bed. I have stuffed soil into my mouth, along with warm strawberries that have lain on the ground for a little too long and will not make the journey home. For hours I have examined the earth's textures, smells and appetites as I remove couch grass roots, flinging them into a pile that will one day become soft, grainy compost.

The intimacy of land connection is very small, sometimes. It's in the ubiquitous blue plastic that I pull from beneath the growing beds. In the hundreds of tiny new gladioli corms that have multiplied beneath the last patch of couch grass on the plot. In the cats, both feral and happily homed, who live in or around the allotment, watching me balefully as I plant, and sometimes, like the foxes, resting on the sun-warmed earth nearby. In the conversations I hold with plot holders about the right way to harvest garlic (ten months in the ground, needs a frost for the cloves to separate), or the invasive nature of comfrey, or how my neighbour was stranded with family in Zimbabwe week after week as her plot foundered during the first Covid lockdown. And how, when she finally returned, months after planting time, the rest of the allotment donated established plants so that she would still have a harvest later on in the year. On allotments, land connection is familiar and yet secret, guarded and deep, open and silent. It is caught up in the lives of a community, and in my life, and in the beings who live on and around each plot.

Words do not do justice to the feeling. The concertina expands and contracts. Small big. Big small.

On a working retreat where I shovel soft, well-rotted leaf mould into old compost bags, one of the trainee gardeners tells me about permaculture's approaches to yield. Yields that might conventionally only have measured the quantity of edible or saleable produce made by an allotment or walled garden or smallholding or farm could also measure the abundance of other gifts: beauty, peace, spaciousness, views, mental well-being, biodiversity. Yield could be measured in the warmth and kinship of two people as they silently heap biomatter into sacks, piling them up to be redistributed around planting beds elsewhere on the wide estate.

Yield is about intimacy too: about the quiet, undramatic contentment that comes from caring for a small patch of land in a community of other people who care for theirs and, by extension, yours. It's true that, over the four years that I've held the key to that portal framed by trees, the quantity, regularity and consistency of the food we've grown on the allotment has increased. There are jars of 2020's preserved runner beans and green-tomato chutney sitting on the shelf in my under-stairs cupboard, waiting to be shared. Our fridge holds frozen French beans from last year's harvest. For Halloween, my part-ner carved a pumpkin bigger than both our heads combined. Strung up over the summer with mesh and hanging from a tall frame, it was a wayfinding landmark between the plots. Now it satisfies small children hunting for sweets. All this is yield, but of a different, more distributed kind.

Inside the allotments there are no barriers and no gates, no walls, no fences. No one who works the land owns the land; consequently no one individual needs to defend their territory. It is astonishing that this model of co-operative, together-but-separate, interdependent growing still exists. It is not a free utopia: subtle, invisible barriers keep an allotment out of reach for many. But once the gate key is in your hand (and you pay your small annual fees, and you continue to grow produce, and you contribute to the general upkeep of the allotments), there are no identity checks, no border controls. The land is not yours, nor will it be unreasonably taken away. What it asks of you is your time, your love, your labour and your care. What it yields is always more than what you give.

My friend R has an allotment a mile away. She has noticed the joy of community in her allotment too, and it is not what you would expect. When R arrived, the allotment society rotavated the plot for her; now she grows courgettes by the barrowful and hands them out to neighbours in the hope that the plenty will be enjoyed for the brief time it makes an appearance. She tells me something else that rings true: many allotmenteers come to their plots to grieve. Not all growing beds are the size of a grave, but the length and width of a manageable patch is often not short of that.

The land will hold you when you are in pain. Grief is the evidence of love; land absorbs it like a sponge, breaks it down into nitrogens and phosphates, wormcasts and mycelium. Grieving is unending and timeless, and land has time for this. Land always has time for slow transformation. The conversations I have with regular allotmenteers always reveal slower stories beneath the infestations and the blight. Stories of long-term injury, accidents, bereavement and loss. Tragedies large and small. Allotments welcome plot holders with chronic illness; so long as there is someone who can do the work, or help with the work, or somehow make a contract with the land so it grows something new, the shape of the body and its capacity are not important. It's not that allotments are accessible as such – for many people they are not, by virtue of all kinds of socio-economic and physical barriers. The spaces between plots are unlikely to be suitable for anything but the most rugged of wheelchairs, for example. But they are capacious of grief and illness, and they do not require recovery. You don't ever have to get 'better' to hold an allotment.

Some plots become unmanageable. Then they are returned to the general pool. Someone else comes to the top of the register. Life goes on. Grief goes on.

The ecologist Mary-Jayne Rust has written about the overpowering grief and joy of learning how to reconnect to nature. She writes, 'A loving relationship with the rest of nature inevitably includes the pain of losing loved ones, or trauma when places or creatures are damaged.'* This is part of what she describes as ecological intimacy. It is the slow process of returning to our place in nature, neither set apart by dominating heroes, nor halted by devastating villains. We are not filaments severed

* Mary-Jayne Rust, 'Ecological Intimacy', in Mary-Jayne Rust and Nick Totton (eds.) *Vital Signs: Psychological Responses to Ecological Crisis* (Taylor & Francis Group, 2012).

from the web of the natural world. Ecological intimacy is about learning how to sew ourselves back into this breathing, moving constellation, without losing a sense of that torn and broken past. We break and we mend. This is how it goes. This is how it can go, still.

There is always grief in reconnection because of what was lost in the meantime. Because of what was lost before my lifetime, which began at a point where irreversible ecological damage had already been under way for centuries, long before the Industrial Revolution, in the name of European empire-building. I carry the grief of previous generations, as well as my own. I also carry my complicity in the environmental breakdown that I see around me. Even on a tiny plot of land. It's a hard thing to admit: shame creeps in when I acknowledge that my early turning over of this plot will likely have destroyed millions of mycelial connections; that digging in wet weather might have irreparably damaged the fine structures of the soil, that when I leave soil bare, especially in the summer, it erodes, impoverished, dust particles flying into the air. But, more importantly, how I live beyond the plot is brought into sharp relief when I am on it. Every time I waste food, every time (and though these have become less frequent) I step on a plane, get in a car or turn up the heating, every day I live under a government intent on revoking even the most basic of environmental and human protections on this small island,

and far beyond its borders. Though allotments have facilitated small household land cultivation for at least a century
or two, maybe longer, hundreds of years of enclosure acts –
land-grabs by the ultrawealthy – had already stolen away the
right to land and to food growing for all. I work the land on
a remnant of social policy implemented as a tiny counterbal-
ance to a vast epoch of aristocratic wealth accumulation, and
the loss of centuries, perhaps millennia, of land knowledge.
Everything is connected.

There may be tiny resistance in cultivating a small, rented
pocket of land, if only to resist the encroachment of land use
for profit. Allotment regulations prohibit the sale of produce,
though it is always acceptable to give it away. And we often
do: fresh, preserved, frozen, pickled. Food for another day. It
is life-affirming to share what we have in abundance. A joy, a
privilege, and an intimate grief.

Big ecological stories are invariably about wild nature: the
wilderness, natural ecosystems that are a far reach from
the urban environments that the majority of the human population inhabits. By 2050, the prediction is that 68 per cent
of the world's population will live in cities.* So what about

---

* United Nations Department of Economic and Social Affairs, '68%
of the world population projected to live in urban areas by 2050, says
UN', 16 May 2018, https://www.un.org/development/desa/en/news/
population/2018-revision-of-world-urbanization-prospects.html.

small nature? Allotments are highly biodiverse, with tiny microclimates that shelter and house every element of the food chain, from microbial life to apex predators. In the urban setting of my home, where a journey to the countryside takes at least an hour, this space of growing, labouring, living alongside the natural world, is where my ecological intimacy comes from on a daily basis. I am not a fully wild creature; nor are the foxes, hedgehogs, bats, feral cats, birds, newts, frogs, fish, insects, invertebrates and other beings with whom I and my fellow allotmenteers share our plots.

I mentioned that failure comes later, didn't I? It came before, too.

In 2019 I experienced a health crisis that consumed me for the best part of a year; more if you consider its run-up and aftermath. The full story probably began a decade earlier. But by then I was in pain daily, on a scale that takes my breath away to remember it. My body and mind failed to hold me, and so I dematerialised a lot of the time, moving closer to becoming particulate matter than I would like to admit. The land held me then. Or rather, it was indifferent. Pain, suffering, death: they are all ecological cycles. Decomposition is what life feeds on. My breakdown, of cataclysmic and therefore deeply mundane proportions, was embraced by my allotment. There was no expectation of repair. Only an invitation to care for these five rods, and the land beyond it. And so that is what I did.

I don't see my own bodymind failures as separate in any way from the rises and falls of the plot, and what lies beyond. Everything is connected. Small big. Big small.

The fine spring and summer of 2020 were the immediate environmental effects of one tiny moment: the world standstill at the outset of the Covid pandemic. Climate remediation is too much to aspire to, and yet for one brief pause the air was clearer. Things were quiet, among the death. Compared with any other form of outdoor activity, allotment access for food growing was relatively uninhibited. It was an extraordinary privilege to have access to this place; even to see other allot-menteers tending their own plots from a distance. Recovering in my slow, blotchy way, I found myself surrounded by others doing the same. Those who were not ill or caring for the sick were often on furlough. Growing seemed a wholly natural place to focus our efforts, and the effects were abundant.

Yield comes in many forms, including silence. Some plots ran wild and fallow at their leisure, because of illness, or caring responsibilities, or death. It would have been a strange cruelty at the height of a global pandemic to dispossess a plot holder of land they were allotted. Abundance is not always counted in vegetables; sometimes it is wild grasses and self-seeded bur-dock, and millions of invertebrates.

By the time something had begun to rebuild, failure crept in, again. In 2021, the initial effects of lockdowns had waned, and the combined impact of a vast economic downturn and an exponential increase in social and financial inequality created a slowdown in allotmenting on our site. Burnout and exhaustion played their part, no doubt – though the dialect of allotmenting tends to acknowledge failure more readily than in other quarters. When I say this, I can only observe what I noticed. Conversations happen only between those who are present. The mood had shifted, time accelerated, and waiting lists jumped in length. It was heart-warming to see new plot holders arrive, and yet new growth was also sporadic. For every new plot holder there is also one on the way out. Allotmenting is incremental, ongoing labour, and in the midst of the grind it is not easy to break ground. A neighbouring plot holder, a professional gardener, struggled to keep his patch under some semblance of order while he laboured relentlessly on other people's gardens. Watch an allotment over time and it carries traces of the world around it in miniature.

Meanwhile a catastrophically wet, cold spring and barely visible summer generated an unstoppable increase in slugs and snails and other voracious mandibles. Vegetable beds were stripped bare of seedlings – even the roots. Nature named its price. On our half-plot, almost everything failed, except for the late-growing tomatoes, which were simply graced by early blight. Allotment growing is an exercise in climate observation – human observation too. Another new neighbour, a chef and the son of an Italian farmer, turned over the plot next to us, which had filled with tall grasses over the slow course of eighteen months. At lightning speed he installed immaculate beds of equally immaculate salad, huge peach-like tomatoes, tall sprays of asparagus. I am still in awe of his discipline, which he holds lightly.

The blast furnace of 2022's summer created extraordinary divergence: peas could not withstand the heat, and I am grateful we planted early, else we'd have had none at all. Potatoes came surprisingly good, and we feasted on lozenges of pink fir apple for months. But so much withered, and watering was worrisome. The absence of hoses on the site came into full perspective: during a hosepipe ban the water butts stayed full. But still, finding ways to reduce water consumption left me wondering about how to grow less thirsty crops. The seasonal swings are now so vast, what will survive one year will wither the next. The last few years have alternated searing heat with downpours, early and late frosts, winds that rip through the plot scattering compost-bin lids and anything not fastened down with hefty bricks. And yet, my neighbours have renewed: luscious beds of artichoke and aubergine, immaculate bushels of Brussels sprouts. People too.

On my allotment I learn about what people leave behind. Not just the allotmenteers around my plot, as we greet each other, half bent over, watering or attending to weeds. Decades, maybe centuries, of people turned this land. Their traces remain. In the twisted metal of greenhouses, several fathoms down, and the train carriages carted off for scrap or for homes. Yet here, in this place, I also learn what people create in their wake. How they care for the land, how they love it, tells me about the multiplicity of land-loving there is to be had. Ruthless weed excision with hand tools; luscious interplanting; green manure rising over the heads of rhubarb. Each one loves the land in a different way. I have much to learn from all of them.

All these constellations of connection are intimate, and they begin very small. Flea beetle punctures. A mouse trail. Ragged leeks. A glut of courgettes. Clay beds and glasshouses. Killing in the name of utopia. War and land-grabs. Grief. Joy. Failure. Renewal.

The connections aren't linear or oppositional. They meander and grow, making queer bedfellows and curious companions. Like me. Like my allotment plot, which loses itself sometimes, and then comes back. Grieves and makes joy. Maybe we all could be like this, in connection with one another and our land. To make our intimacy our strength.

ALLOTMENTS
ARE ANOMALIES

Rebecca Schiller

Katy is in my way.

She stands on the north-westerly shore where the air is anger and ice. The wind slaps her cheeks, whips strands of dark hair from her bun to make ringlets and stiffens her striped apron with salt spray starch.

Her arms are folded. Big with work. Muscles of seaweed, boulder clay and peat press her skin against the roughness of her faded clothes.

If she moved, you would hear a slight scratching noise.

But she doesn't move.

No matter how hard I try to get her to budge, Katy refuses to do so much as blink. She is stubborn; remaining here where surely she doesn't belong: in this piece, in my head, in the way.

So, this is where we start: Katy. A tilted chin, a pattern of freckles and a whiff of stubborn nanny goat.

My father-in-law Allan is visiting. We sit around our old oak table in our new larch home and pass polite questions around with the bread basket.

It is the first day of his first trip to the croft that became ours late this summer, when we moved over six hundred miles from a smallholding in Kent to the north-east of Scotland. Now it is autumn, and though there are still leaves on our birches and rowans, their multicoloured zing has faded and the wind knocks them off with ease.

Over lunch, he asks about work and I explain that I am writing about allotments. 'Or trying to,' I confess, guiltily thinking of this page, full of disconnected half-thoughts and stilted dead ends.

The trouble – I try to explain – is that I feel out of place here. I don't know allotments. I've never had one, never hankered after one, never even spent much time in one. And though I do know something about working a plot of land; attempting to turn soil into food and flowers, allotments are different – particular – and I worry I have nothing to say.

The other trouble – and I don't even try to explain this – is that I am all jagged half-questions and gaps at the moment.

Disorientated by so much change and unsure how to recalibrate, I have no arguments and no answers. I look for a way into allotments and trip over my bootlaces face first onto another path.

When I try to write something earthy about the land, I find myself waist deep in the Atlantic Ocean instead.

There is a wall on this beach, and it is breathing in and out. It is a wall of women, each brick a Katy, a Màiri or an Anna. The cold must be a fresh shock every time it hits their lungs, yet they do not so much as twitch; not even as the Landlord's boats appear and the men bob into the blue bay like lost buoys.

Katy/Ceitid – daughter-of-Mary, crofter of Coigach, ringleader of this resistance – why are you here where you don't belong: in this essay, in this book? Why won't you stand aside and let me pass?

I used to take troublesome questions and tangled thoughts to my garden. I dug and weeded and sowed until my brain agreed to cooperate. But this new hillside has only the memory of cultivation; long submerged under wildness and heather and fungi and gorse and broom and lichen and woodland and wonder. I do not have a garden here. Not yet.

For the first time in my adult life I have a straight choice: put my hands in the soil or keep them clean.

In every home until now I have inherited some sort of growing space to guiltily ignore or engage with. A tiny courtyard with a few pots, a small lawn with curved borders and, in my last house, a proper gardener's garden with vegetable beds, fruit cages and herbaceous borders.

It is odd to have nothing to prune, water or feed. Nothing from the plot to add to my long 'to do' list. It is a rest, a relief. It is exactly what I need after an exhausting and difficult few years.

I do not want to make a garden, let alone an allotment-style plot; not yet, not now. I overdid in every direction in my last place and all I want is a little more softness and a little more sleep. My knuckles are arthritic. My back protests.

Yet something, someone, somewhere keeps pulling me back to the idea despite myself. I find myself browsing a Scottish fruit tree website, tracing the outline of raised beds over a piece of gently sloping grass and thumbing through the envelopes of saved seeds I brought with me, presumably in case of some unlikely gardening emergency.

The feeling is of compulsion, not desire. The urge to get started is irrational, unnecessary, inconvenient and stupid. What's the rush, after all? It feels like a kind of mania – a horticultural Stockholm syndrome – a magnetic pull towards the earth. A duty? A tic? A symptom? Whatever it is, it feels as if the choice to get back to the garden might not be mine to make after all.

The boats get closer to the shore, the Landlord's men are now able to see the sand turning to stones turning to grass as the beach sweeps up and becomes the hill and the hill becomes the wall of women. The men tell themselves their nausea is from the shift of the waves, but it is not. They see Katy and the others and, though they don't quite know why, the sight turns their stomachs and pulls the colour from their cheeks.

This is the time of the Highland Clearances. 1852 on the north-west of Scotland peninsula: Coigach – or A'Chòigeach as Katy likely calls it. The men in the boats are coming from the Estate to serve eviction notices for eighteen families who have lived and worked here for generations. The Landowner wants the crofters out. Money can be made more swiftly and in larger volume if they are forced to move, and so Katy and Co. are to be told to heft themselves to less valuable land and start life anew.

The same thing is happening repeatedly across the Highlands. The officials come and the families must move to another, rougher hillside – or over the ocean to a supposedly new world. There have been some protests but almost all have failed. The landlords win, the families disperse, the old croft houses are abandoned, and the gardens and strips of arable land are reclaimed by nature or nibbled by hordes of hungry sheep.

The crofters of Coigach are no different. They don't own this land that they grow and live on. They should lose this fight. They should be quaking in their tatty old boots. They shouldn't have a leg to stand on.

And yet there she is, Katy, standing firmly on both legs and still refusing to get out of the way.

'I had an allotment once.'

It is the second day of my father-in-law's visit when he drops this unexpected jewel into conversation, and I pounce excitedly.

It was the seventies, he explains, in north London. He is sketchy on the detail; not remembering exactly when, for how long or even quite where the allotment was. The only thing he recalls clearly is 'digging'. He says the word with a half-shudder and a disbelieving shake of his head; looking off to the right as if at someone else entirely – someone who temporarily took leave of their senses sometime around 1976.

As he talks, his body seems to recall a sensation I know

well. The jerk when you attempt to make the edge of your spade cut into the ground and discover that matted stems and roots can form an almost supernaturally powerful forcefield that spades just bounce off.

When my father-in-law took on the allotment, it was completely overgrown, the earth shielded from view by a thickness of grass, docks, nettles and brambles. He describes lifting and hauling for days on end just to get to the point where soil appeared. Then there would have been the relentless work of sowing, pricking out, planting, watering, netting, feeding and harvesting. Thorns, stings and splinters. Heavy, sharp things that were angled into roots and would not give in no matter how hard they were pulled. He would have strained his shoulder muscles, muddied and chipped his fingernails and developed a perma-ache in his lower back. And just when he thought he was nearly finished, it would have started to bloody rain again.

The kind of small-scale growing you do on allotments, crofts and smallholdings is always hard work. Your body is required to be the tractor, the plough and the muck-spreader. You have to put that body outside and move it around in all weathers, all the while pretending the supermarket does not exist.

For most of us it is no longer about survival or self-sufficiency. It is usually a more time-consuming, difficult, less reliable and more expensive way to eat. And it is often hard to achieve. Just finding a plot or making it to the top of an allotment waiting list takes persistence.

Growing like this, these days, is something you should need a persuasive reason to engage in. You should require a real passion and purpose – a desire, a calling, to do it. And yet when I ask my father-in-law why he took on the allotment, he tells me he doesn't know. He can't remember. He has no idea – nor can he say why he carried on doing it after the back-breaking reality hit.

'I'm not sure I even grew very much,' he adds, as if he has been hypnotised, 'apart from kohlrabi. I grew quite a lot of kohlrabi.' Though how and why he decided on this odd crop he doesn't recall either.

Badenscallie beach is more full of human life than it has ever been. The crofters, the Landlord's men, the children lurking in the long grass trying not to catch their parents' attention. A baby crying somewhere, swaddled not quite into submission. And everyone's face grim.

The men try to serve the eviction notices, but Katy refuses to take them. The Officer and the Sheriff and someone else – who might have been a lawyer – pale further as the atmosphere becomes charged.

The women will not get out of the way. They will not take these eviction notices. They will not leave Coigach. They refuse to take their hands out of this difficult earth. They will not shift their feet from its familiar tussocks.

The men look at each other as if they can't understand the women's words. 'What?' Their crumpled brows seem to say. 'We don't get it. This doesn't make sense. This isn't how this is supposed to go.'

Then the smell of burning paper. Later, Katy will remember the feeling of smoke scratching at the back of her nostrils and the surprise of the bright flash of flame. But she can never quite untangle exactly what happened: who put a flame to the eviction notices, who raised their voice first, whether she was at the very front of the living wall as they dismantled themselves brick by brick to become a throng and encircle the Officer?

What she does recall is the familiar feeling of digging: digging in. Her body humming with adrenalin but the inside of her head remaining surprisingly quiet. Everything blurring and then there he is, the Officer, back in his boat bobbing away now and stripped completely naked. His skin is mottled purple, each follicle a little Everest, and his teeth clatter together like wheels on a loose track.

Serves him right.

*

Kohlrabi isn't a crop that I have ever grown or knowingly eaten and I read that it looks 'something like a Sputnik in vegetable form'. Its name and this exotic description have made it sound like an alien life form. Yet when I look at the images on my computer screen, I'm comforted to recognise wavy-edged leaves and see that it's just a little brassica. *Kohlrabi*: a very ordinary sort of swede-broccoli, dressed up as something from outer space.

A *sputnik* is also a gentler and more familiar word than its spiky sounds suggest. It is simply the Russian for *satellite*; the prefix 's' translating as 'with' and the 'putnik' body of the word meaning 'traveller'. *S-putnik: fellow-traveller*. Sputnik-1, the world's first satellite, was sent into orbit on 4 October 1957. The giant kohlrabi was launched into space from the Soviet Union's chosen site in southern Kazakhstan and orbited the earth 1,440 times before eventually burning up in the Earth's atmosphere.

In 1962, four years and 1,500 miles from Sputnik-1's launch, my father-in-law enlarged his own orbit, travelling from England to the USSR during the Cold War. His unusual journey was the next phase in a career that had begun nearly a decade previously, when he was just ten years old. I have looked at the black-and-white photos of that day many times, though quite why I can't tell you. There he is: making his professional debut only two years into playing. All big eyes, pulled-up knee socks, scratchy-looking shorts and family resemblance. He could be my husband or my son in 1950s costume, except for the backdrop of the musicians of the Hallé Orchestra, Sir John Barbirolli's baton and the audience slack-jawed with awe.

That is the thing about my father-in-law. He is a pianist. Not the back-room bar kind. Not the Sunday-ballet-lesson kind. Not even the revolving door of little pupils clutching dog-eared sheet music kind. My father-in-law is a bone fide genius. A child prodigy concert pianist with rare magic in his hands. He was the first British pianist to win a scholarship to study at the Moscow Conservatory, arriving in the Soviet Union as Sputnik-23 set off on its journey to Mars.

In the days after his visit to our croft a new image papers the inside of my head. It jostles for space with glimpses of Katy resisting eviction despite having so little power and with imaginings of the garden that I shouldn't want. This latest image is also of dissonance: of his precious, muddy hands against the white keys of a piano. A man whose fingers and arms and back were everything, yet who risked them in the earth and the brambles for a reason he cannot remember or maybe never even knew.

Here, in the Bermuda Triangle between these three images, I begin to spot a pattern that is sharp and persuasive.

*

I have form for being drawn to this kind of thinking, despite many other easier, more rational alternatives. One Tuesday in my early twenties I was busy cursing myself for following a similar thread and ending up in a seminar room giving a wobbly voiced presentation on wartime strategy and tactics to a largely male audience – many of whom claimed to have been in the military.

The year before I'd been finishing a nice, logical English Literature degree during which I became obsessed with war poetry and plays. There was something in wartime literature that I wondered about and wanted, but I wasn't at all clear what it was or how to begin to get to it. On a hunch that I might need to go into the subject from a different angle, I set up camp next door in the famous King's College London War Studies department.

Poking about in the Imperial War Museum, I discovered something that seemed entirely mad. Since the First World War, in a series of schemes that have evolved into something that still exists, there has been an official war art programme in Britain. It sounds as crazy to me now as it did then. When the British armed forces are significantly engaged in a conflict, it is someone's actual job to find and deploy not only soldiers and tanks and bulletproof vests, but a visual artist. Moreover, the artist's role is not to document the conflict – we have war reporters, photographers and human rights NGOs for that. They are there to make an artistic response to that war – to interpret and engage with it – something that humans have been doing unofficially in times of conflict as far back in history as we can trace.

Within the constraints of the societal framework in which I grew up, this didn't really make sense. Art is a nice-to-have extra. Writing a lovely afterthought. Creativity something that society values, funds and consumes only to a point – as leisure, luxury or ephemera. Following that logic, it should be one of the first things to disappear in times of privation and stress. And yet the very opposite turns out to be true.

War makes poets and painters. Literature expands and changes when caught in crossfire and new artistic movements are born from the battlefield. Here, in the most challenging, perilous, traumatic, expensive, pared-back-to-the-fundamental-basics-of-existence times, humans are compelled to pick up a pencil and scribble a poem or make a sketch in their mud- and blood-spattered notebooks.

I was drawn to war literature and art because they felt like anomalies and I was sure that the vibrating dissonance that surrounds anomalies should never be ignored. The official war art scheme drew me in because it seemed to be a super-anomaly in the slow, heavy bureaucracy of conflict.

An almost accidental, left-behind clue that late-capitalist society had forgotten to kick into the dusty darkness under the bed.

I let it pull me in because to me its existence was government-funded proof of what I had always instinctively felt and what art and literature tells anyone who will listen: human creativity is more important than the framework we are told we exist within allows for it to be. It is fundamental to us. Unavoidable. Intrinsic. A survival instinct that we ignore at our peril. And the places where it exists, despite every reason for it not to, are desperately important. They are the locations of insight, progress and deep remembering; suggestions of another, better, truer way to look at things. Good stuff hiding beneath.

It is midwinter now and the moles have been busy turning my new ground over. They appear whenever I move my grazing animals off a section of land, seeming to prefer the short grass. This morning a fresh pile of beautiful, soft soil has appeared on top of the foot-deep snow. Almost buried under the drifts are pots I filled with the contents of earlier molehills and then planted up with spring bulbs. My first attempt at gardening here on the croft should result in daffodils, tulips, hyacinths, snowdrops and crocus before too long – though it seems unlikely in the thick January cold.

Everything is white and quiet outside but on my desk there's a flash of loud primrose yellow; a small booklet called *The Promised Land*. Published in 1974 by the Strollamus Crofters Defence Committee, its pages detail the battle that another generation of crofters faced to stay on their land. I turn to the beginning where, picked out in large letters, is the start of a sentence: 'The Highlanders have been held by their land, but . . .'

I set this sentence against Katy, who is back on the shore at Badenscallie. Bad an Sgalaidh: place in the hollow. It is another year and another season for her. Summer. Sunlight stretching across time like clingfilm, keeping the day fresh for eighteen hours or more.

She and her husband work the long days moving stones. Since I last saw her, Katy's been further roughened and toughened by these stones. Her face is tanned, her hair is lighter, her palms are more callused, and she walks with a slight stoop thanks to the constant bending.

They are building the walls of their new house, perched on the western edge of the world in a flood zone – just outside the Estate-land boundary, which she, as former ringleader of a successful resistance, is no longer allowed to cross.

Yes, the crofters of Coigach were successful. They didn't move and the crofts still exist today. And Katy stayed too, despite being banned from living on much of the island. Despite the promise of water lapping over her doorstep and flowing into her new house during spring tides. She stays, even though staying is a crazy, nonsensical thing to do.

Katy is a war poem. She shouldn't persist but she does. She doesn't make sense in the current framework. She doesn't own her land. It doesn't make her any money. She has suffered for it and will suffer still. And there she is, moving rocks and getting in the way.

And if Katy is a war poem then surely my father-in-law on his allotment is the official war art scheme. His precious, genius hands are feted around the world. He is careful with himself – he has to be. And yet, somehow, the grunt work of an allotment pulled him in and held him close for a while.

It is the dissonance again that gets me. The *why* of it. The same *why* I have in me as I look at my land and wonder what it is that makes me want to pick up a spade and choose a flattish south-facing part to exhaust myself into. It doesn't make sense in the current framework, but it keeps happening – in defiance of logic and time, and how much easier it is to buy food than grow it.

I turn this nonsense over, hoping for something profound. Something that transcends the structure through which we have learned to understand the world. Something beyond the idea that growing some food on an allotment or a veg patch is a nice, wholesome hobby. Good for the planet. Good for our mental health. A little indulgent, a touch irrelevant. An anachronism. Something that could be cut out in lean times.

In this anomalous, seemingly irrational, stubborn pursuit there must be something transcendent and important, otherwise I am a genuine lunatic and so, I hazard a guess, are you. In this ground, in this allotment or that croft, there has to be a clue as to who we really are and how the world really works. There must be something here in the defiance of all the bullshit that we are told and that we tell ourselves.

I wish I knew what it was. I wish I could tell you.

All I have for now is the beginnings of a hunch.

In his 1942 war poem 'Naming of Parts', Henry Reed looks sideways at an ordinary piece of military training – the naming of parts of an Enfield rifle – and renders it absurd and nonsensical. Reed takes the gun and the suggestion of what will be done with it – piece by named piece – and sets it against the garden and nature quietly at work: flowers springing into bloom, bees busy pollinating. What seemed to make sense a moment ago in the context of the war effort is instantly transformed. The gun lunacy. The bees sane.

I read the poem again now thinking that there must be a way to do the same thing in reverse. To take the pull I feel to growing and sowing and render it sensical and important. To find a frame through which this feeling of being held by the land – against my will at times – is normal and everything else we do and say and think and feel, a sham.

For even though there are sunny days and absolute magic in the moment of germination. Even though nothing tastes like a cauliflower that you once held in your hands as a round, black speck of seed, I would not do this if I didn't have to. But I have to. I am like Katy. I cannot move out of the way.

Maybe we are incubating something important in these nonsensical, somewhat counter-capitalist structures. A little piece of DNA that we might need to hold on to, kept in play by allotments, crofts and back garden veg patches?

A piece that means that when we stray from her, the land can jerk us back. I feel it. I am sure Katy felt it. I wonder if, subconsciously perhaps, my father-in-law felt it too. The tug on the toddler reins from a parent who sees we are too close to danger and pulls us sharply back to the safety of their arms.

I have this thought. I write it down. And somewhere in the North Atlantic of my mind Katy finally steps aside and lets me through. The air is still anger and ice, but she is no longer in my way. I have a spade and a nose for nonsense and, above all, I know how to dig.

OLD BOYS AND
HIDDEN WOMEN

JC Niala

I don't look as though I belong on an allotment site. My clothes are a little too clean and I prefer trainers to boots, which any serious allotmenteer will tell you are impractical. Over the thirty-six months that I carried out doctoral fieldwork on allotment sites across Oxford, I gave up trying to appear like a 'typical' plot owner and instead focused on the benefits of being an obvious 'incomer'. Incomers are outsiders and as someone who has, one way or another, been an outsider all her life, I know that people tell outsiders things they would not tell anyone else. The stakes are low when you leave your secrets with outsiders; they will keep these revelations to themselves and even if they do share them, it won't be with anyone who *matters*.

I was on these allotment sites to carry out ethnographic fieldwork, which is predicated on two things. The first is being able to observe, and the second that people will open up to you. It also helps if you have an 'in'. One of mine is that I grew up around gardens and gardening. I know the language and I have even been known to produce harvests. My other 'in' is my African upbringing. In most African cultures, children are trained from a very young age to listen to and engage respectfully with elders. And there is a very special type of elder responsible for the fact that we can still grow at allotment sites across Britain today – the 'old boys'.

Now, I should say that the term 'old boy' is not derogatory. Old boys call themselves and others 'old boys', and are special for being the only type of allotmenteer with this kind of specific designation. Mention 'old boy' to anyone on an allotment site and they will immediately know who you mean. They are stereotypically white, English and working-class. Perhaps the sort of man who holds up his trousers with bailer twine and is considered to be (and perhaps considers himself to be) 'salt of the earth'. Regardless, he certainly commands a particular status on allotment sites. As one old boy, John, told me, 'Now that I am an old boy, no one can tell me what to do.' Old boys are revered for their growing knowledge, are understood to hold particular freedoms available to no one else on the site and are slightly feared for their judgements, doled out advisedly. I took it as a compliment when I was told off by one old boy for popping onto the site that morning for only half an hour. There were a clear number of jobs that needed doing but all I could manage on that particular day was a quick water.

The 'old boy' in question was having none of my 'better than nothing' approach. It meant he cared enough about me (or the patch of land I was growing on) to tell me to make the time for it. 'Seedlings,' he told me (I was trying to nurture a few), 'are like babies, you know.' The old boys' first allegiance is to the land and the allotment site – your plot and your produce tells them all they need to know – but back in the day there was some resistance as to who was allowed to engage with these spaces in the first place.

On a crisp late autumn afternoon, as we sipped tea in her kitchen, Peggy, now retired, told me about a stereotypical old boy who for a time ran the allotment site where she has had a plot for over forty years. 'He was a very nice guy,' she said, 'but he wasn't really interested in talking to anyone other than guys.' Peggy described the difficulty she initially had in securing a plot, being told by him that the site was full. A public-sector worker for decades, Peggy was astute at reading people and immediately sent her husband down to enquire instead. He was immediately given a choice of six plots, selecting the one he thought Peggy would like best. Her husband has never since cultivated the allotment in all the decades they've had it, and yet it is his name that has remained on the lease ever since.

If Peggy had told this story before I started my research, I wouldn't have understood what she said next. 'You owe a lot to the people who wouldn't give me an allotment,' she told me, 'because actually, one way or another, they kept the sites going.

Terrible means they used to do it, and some of them were terrible. Nevertheless, they kept them going.' And she's right. During the post-war era, convenience foods had become commonplace and growing your own food was no longer considered a leisure activity. The rising value of urban land coupled with many plots' disuse and disrepair meant that, in Peggy's words, 'Allotments were really disappearing at a huge rate of knots.' By the sixties, the situation was alarming enough that the government ordered a committee of enquiry.

Harry Thorpe, Professor of Geography at the University of Birmingham at the time, produced a report in the early seventies that proposed a transformation of what he called these 'horticultural slums' into leisure gardens. This is part of the reason that the full name of the National Allotment Society remains the National Society for Allotments and Leisure Gardeners. Setting aside Thorpe's offensive description of allotments, his words had minimal effect on increasing allotment numbers, even as the kinds of reformed spaces he had in mind (though they did perhaps unwittingly predict the gentrification of allotments from the noughties onwards). And so it was left to the old boys to carry out the spadework that has seen allotments survive and go on to thrive in the present day. Their constant daily presence on these plots was the groundwork required to ensure that they did not simply vanish from the British landscape. Sites that were seen as not having active allotmenteering were most vulnerable to being closed down and developed – so many old boys took on an extra plot, some even two or three, to keep sites alive until demand grew.

That's the thing. In their own ways, these old boys really care – about the land, about growing and about their individual specific interests, liking to connect to people *through* those interests. But they have to know that those interests matter to you too. That was the trickier part of building a rapport with them during my time on Oxfordshire's plots, but I was lucky that I would often go to the allotments in the early morning. A few people with jobs would be there too, rushing through with small chunks of time before heading to their desks. But the other early-morning arrivals, many of whom would settle in for a large part of the day, were the old boys.

On my first early morning on a site that I will call Swardland, I heard Eric, a spry eighty-nine-year-old, shout as he arrived. Even though we would grow alongside each other for over twelve months, I never understood what it was that Eric hollered. It was a cross between a call and a salutation. I made my own loud noise back and followed Eric into the communal allotment building. Once there, Eric was joined by a few other of the old fellas smoking their pipes, even though it was (strictly speaking) against the rules. When I told them about my research into allotments, they were barely interested – land was for actively engaging with, not theorising – yet when

I mentioned that I was also a war historian everything changed. Eric had been in Libya and others eagerly told me where they had been stationed, whether army or navy. After that, whenever I joined them, they would talk to me, share their experiences in bite-sized pieces. I was careful not to outstay my welcome, though if I'd spent, say, an hour at my plot before needing to head off elsewhere, they would also ask me warmly: 'Where the bloody hell do you think you're going?'

One clear spring morning at Swardland, I stood absorbed by the daffodils lining the edges of the allotment building and the adjacent lawn. Out of the early stillness, Eric approached me, and even though the world was yet to face the Covid pandemic, he instinctively maintained a small distance between us. Despite the march of time beginning to show, Eric always brushed off any concerns about his well-being with a quip about his 'aches and pains'. With both of us looking out over the serene vista of the farmer's fields in the distance, Eric broke the silence. 'I planted those,' he said, nodding down at the daffodils. 'Thank you,' I replied, and smiled. He hadn't planted them for me, but the beauty he had added felt personal.

Eric went on to paint a vivid picture of a bygone era, when he had adorned the site with flowers and when most of the allotmenteers were men. The plots, he recalled, were delineated by well-kept pathways. They were productive yet had an aesthetic order; they were, as another old boy once put it to me, as 'clean as a whistle'. The productiveness was in part borne out of necessity. It was not like 'nowadays' when people can get food easily whatever the season. When something was harvested, another crop was immediately planted in its wake, with the only pause being for compost. Yet I was still intrigued by the flowers, and I asked why he had stopped planting them. 'It's not like it used to be, is it?' Eric mused. In my African culture, when an elder says something like this, it's an invitation into their memories. It's impolite to brush it off or to claim ignorance of that past. So, honouring that tradition, I responded with a gentle, 'No, it's not, is it?'

What followed was a conversation coloured by both nostalgia and a deep sense of care. Eric mourned the visual shifts on the site. The choices people once made in plotting their gardens, the materials they used and the plants they grew had collectively given shape to the image of a quintessential English allotment. And some of that had changed in the intervening years, and was continuing to change. Nevertheless, Eric still had a quiet influence on Swardland, even if he was no longer liberally adorning it with flowers. He was an unofficial member of the allotment committee; everyone knew his opinion carried the most weight. Yet there was a curious sense of a baton being passed here too, and of it loosely being based on gender. Increasing numbers of middle-aged women (quite a number of them middle-class) are now at the helm of these groups. When I raised this, many of the old boys said that they'd done their time, with some adding that 'to be fair' the women seemed to be making a better job of it. Women routinely responded that things needed 'sorting out' and that they were the ones to do it.

Aside from these generalisations, something I sensed or saw on a few sites and that does seem to be playing out across the country, is that there are now more women cultivating on allotment sites across Britain than men. Dr Tilly Collins and Ellen Fletcher from Imperial College London conducted a nationwide study, revealing that women now occupy 63.7 per cent of London's 24,883 allotment plots. Something has definitely shifted. However, with careful consideration, it seems that even this figure is an underestimate. I met a young woman in her thirties who grows only cut flowers so she can spread joy by giving them to people and who shares her plot with a few friends. I interviewed a female allotmenteer who splits her plot with her twin sister. I met a middle-aged woman who works for an international NGO whose friend uses her plot whenever she is travelling. In all these cases, only one name is on the tenancy. The more digging I did, the more I found a pattern: women across Oxford were sharing their allotment plots and other women – significant numbers – were working them, hidden in plain sight. The world of allotments is no longer a male stronghold, but a space where many women grow. And, perhaps surprisingly to some, this isn't a new phenomenon.

Women have been growing on allotment sites for at least a century, often escaping official records. As with so many other skills and occupations, it is at times of national crisis that their stories can be more easily brought into the light. The outbreak of the First World War was a turning point. With a significant portion of the male population conscripted for the war, Britain faced a dire food shortage. To address this issue, the lesser-known DORA, or Defence of the Realm Act, empowered local authorities to repurpose unused plots of land for allotments. As a result, women were thrust forwards, stepping up to tend the fields and ensure the nation's sustenance. Many took over allotments too, sowing, reaping crops, breaking the stereotype that this was a man's domain. Yet when soldier husbands returned from war, many of these women, who had developed strong relationships with the land, did not want to give up their plots. The Rowntree family, known for the Quaker ethics practised in their businesses, resolved this tension in a unique way. In 1917, they formally offered women the opportunity to become plot holders, creating more allotments so that these women would not have to give up the space they had so carefully tended.

Nevertheless, it is much harder to trace the histories of women on allotment sites than for their male counterparts, and clues have to be put together through other forms. The collections at the Garden Museum, for example, show some beautiful photographs of women on allotments at the turn of the twentieth century, flowers and implements in hand. In a comic postcard of the allotments movement of the First World War, in a long line of people marching forwards with garden tools, there is a woman in blue feathered hat and yellow dress pushing a buggy – her baby brandishing a trowel – her two other children grabbing onto her skirts and scowling. So too in those old photographs, the women are frequently holding children aloft. I recognise these women in their present-day counterparts. For two years I cultivated alongside a mother who always came to the allotment with her young sons. Her meticulous terraced plot on the sloping site had parts that were used as a playground. A toy lorry was just as easily found among the rows of vegetables as a spade. For the first twenty-two months that I knew her, I assumed she was a single mother. I was wrong. One day her husband came to drop off some supplies when she wasn't there. Having never seen him before, I protectively went over to find out what he was doing. He told me what I already knew, that he would never usually come down here because 'this was her place'. The key difference was she brought her children with her, whereas those old boys I interviewed did not. I can attest to the fact that although wonderful and nourishing in more ways than the obvious, allotmenteering is hard work. And although women are today much more visible than in times past, what remains hidden are the expectations women either carry or have placed on them alongside that growing, including simultaneous caring duties.

Yet one key aspect of the allotment as a family space is the passing on of knowledge. Both John and Mike, old boys with plots adjoining my own in Oxfordshire, shared their regrets at not having taught their children to allotmenteer. They both confessed that their plots had been a sanctuary as their children were growing up. Somewhere they could keep for themselves between the challenges of hard work and busy home lives. John, however, was trying to make up for lost time by involving his grandchildren. I witnessed and experienced myself something else that no old boy I knew would ever brag about, but that had its own beauty. When clueless younger people started on their first plot, the chaps would frequently find quiet ways to help, lending tools and carefully giving advice. Just as they and the old boys that had come before them had cared for the land, ensuring its survival for the next generation, they were now passing on those skills to others to do the same.

A delicate dance is occurring with the passage of time and this break and part repair of inter-generational knowledge. By the time I finished my thirty-six months of fieldwork, Eric had died. So too had many of his old boy counterparts across the country. As the wheel of time turns, a new chapter emerges, quietly penned by the once hidden women of the allotments. Unrecognised for too long, hidden women are now stepping into the light. The legacy of these cherished allotments continues to flourish, evolving with each successive generation, with hidden women not only preserving a vital part of Britain's cultural heritage, but also redefining it in their own unique way.

SPACE TO GROW: WOMEN AND ALLOTMENTS

Alice Vincent

The allotments were tucked away in the ribcage of the village, further on from the graveyard, behind the wire fences of the playground, just above the fields that still wore their ridges and furrows from centuries before. When I was a child, they were steeped in vague mystery, a place where adults grew things. We were country kids who had free rein of public footpaths and fields and a firm understanding of other people's land. The allotments straddled this divide: not land that belonged to anyone as much as it was on loan. The only things that seemed to come out of there were offerings of vegetables and rumours about what the local teenagers had, or had not, done. What unfolded inside the allotments was a greater enigma yet.

I'm not sure I ever went into those allotments, and I moved away long before I began to understand plants on my own terms. Perhaps they were formative in my subsequent relation-ship with these spaces, so hallowed for so many people. But what I do know is that I still find allotments somehow forbid-den, wildly beguiling and inherently alluring. When I am on them I always feel as if I am a visitor, that these plots are akin to outdoor living rooms and that I should tread carefully if not take my shoes off entirely. Lives and appetites can be extracted from their offerings – not necessarily the produce but the lack thereof, whether the beds are laid out neatly or left to unfurl, whether there is a greenhouse, or a water butt, or a variety of composting mechanisms, ramshackle or otherwise.

A few years ago now I pursued a question that took me into dozens of people's growing spaces: why do you grow? I asked it of women and hundreds of them replied. Over the internet, while the world was locked down and anxious in the midst of a pandemic, I heard stories of grief and resilience, power and motherhood, joy and protest and creation. When I could, I visited some of these women's growing spaces, and it was on a blustery early-March afternoon that I was let in through the padlocked gate of Vimbai's plot, one of dozens on a large field of allotments that clung to the hard shoulder of London's North Circular.

We were the only people there; it was a weekday, and after the golden spring of 2020, the following winter was mean. Vimbai – who was short inside her workwear, wore her hair cropped close and laughed readily – was the first to admit her plot was a work in progress; she'd been granted access to it only just over a year earlier. Already, though, there were signs of industry: neat beds laden with dark compost, which she'd hauled across the allotments in 80-litre bags after waiting on the site all day for a delivery. Half a dozen compost bins to avoid having to do that again. The beginnings of little paths. We sat on two plastic chairs, the kind you might find in a school, but she had dreams of painting the shed she'd inherited with the plot Forest Green.

This was her second allotment plot; its predecessor had been 'very whimsical, a woodland forest thing' in the shadow of Eltham Palace. Riddled with couch grass and home to an oak tree, it was a beautiful but ultimately insurmountable challenge. But then Vimbai and her partner moved to Barnet, at the top end of the Northern Line, and managed to get a place at an allotment within a matter of weeks.

She started growing here after spending three months in Zimbabwe, where she grew up, setting up a garden that she never saw flourish. She's lived in the UK since she was a teenager, but having an allotment has allowed her to reacquaint herself with the British seasons as a gardener. 'We have such a short growing season, you kinda have to move quickly. Which is different from at least growing up in Zimbabwe where you could get away with growing things for most of the year.'

Similarly, growing food has given her a new perspective on it: 'I hate peas normally, but I grew peas and used them as allotment snacks. Very few made it home. But I started collecting some in a little bag to put in a risotto; I'd look at my three peas and I'm like, "Let's put you away." Joy was when I had enough for a pea risotto,' Vimbai tells me; it's easy to believe her, it's shining through her face.

Over the past year Vimbai's come to know the allotment's community. She had a container garden at home, but she said it wasn't the same. 'It's so friendly. My partner has always asked why don't we just get a big garden. But I always say no. I like the allotment vibe of people giving me extra tomatoes they've grown and stuff like that,' she says. 'I wouldn't give that up.' As a Black queer woman, an immigrant who works as a civil servant in Westminster, Vimbai says she's lived a life 'of being in spaces where people like me don't usually go'. By contrast, the allotment has been surprisingly welcoming. 'I could always find something to relate to the other people in the allotment,' Vimbai says. 'I'll be on the allotment, you'll be on the allotment. It's easy to get on with people.'

If I learned anything from asking why women grew, it's that everyone has different, deeply rooted reasons for going to ground. Some things, though, were universal: a need for space and a need for control – two things that women, societally, are often deprived of. Growing offers us a means of both.

But allotments seem to invite in something for women that other growing spaces don't, and that's communion: Vimbai tended to her plot with her partner. I've since heard of allotment plots being shared between women, the domestic duties of the home making sole control of one unthinkable. In turn, these have become spaces of sisterhood, which hold far more than the produce they offer.

I'm often asked if I have, or if I'd take, an allotment. Somehow it feels like a grubby confession to say I wouldn't particularly want one right now. I live in Brixton – the nearest, even if I was to wait out the decades-long list, is a thirty-minute bus ride away. In truth, I don't feel that I'm in an allotment time of my life. They are hungry, beloved things, demanding our thought and physical labour, our weekend hours, our drought-based panic. I could not give a plot what it would need, and that feels unfair when it could be giving so much to someone else.

One day, though, I might join the ranks. Become an allotment person, meet someone I'd never have encountered otherwise and garden alongside them. Grow allotment snacks and take some home for a risotto. Feel a very particular kind of joy spread across my face.

CULTIVATING COMMUNITY

Sui Searle

I arrive at the community garden one morning to find the team clearing a bed that is going to be used to grow cut flowers. They're already part-way through so I grab a fork and join in for the last third. Bed cleared, our next job is to shift the remains of the garden compost from the 'To Use' bay, covering the freshly cleared bed with a thick layer of mulch ready for planting. This will then free up the space for us to turn over the adjacent bay of partially composted plant material into the newly emptied one, and so on, to help speed up the process. There is never a shortage of work to be done in the garden.

A familiar group of us meets at the same time every week, though this doesn't mean that everyone always comes. It's very relaxed. On some occasions there might be a relatively large group of up to ten of us. On others, like today, there are three of us working here: Lisa, Jan and myself. Jan recently picked up a back injury, from which she is still recovering, so Lisa and I do the work of shovelling together and taking it in turns to barrow, while Jan barrows without having to shovel.

I have overdressed, wearing both a wool jumper and rain jacket, and find myself heating up rapidly. It had looked to be threatening rain, after a pretty miserable run of autumn weather and big floods in parts of the country, but it turns out to be very mild and dry. Gradually I peel off the layers.

As we work we chat about making kefir. Jan has just bought some kefir grains and tells us about her new, tentative adventures in making her own fermented milk. None of us has tried doing it before so we're intrigued to hear about the process. Before we know it, the three of us have finished mulching the 12-metre-long bed. Satisfied with our morning's efforts, we break for tea.

In the two years I've been coming to this community garden, there have been plenty of similar activities where we've made light work as a team, from shifting mountains of compost, re-skinning a polytunnel, seed sowing, planting out and harvesting, to putting together veg boxes, weeding, clearing overgrown areas, sorting through accumulated junk, earthing up potatoes, creating new beds, digging trenches for a new irrigation system and much more.

Not only does it make big, potentially daunting and arduous tasks feel surmountable, but it's fun, companionable and so much quicker too. Everyone brings different skills, strengths, interests and ideas with them, which adds to the richness of the experience and our problem-solving capabilities.

One of the things I find most generative though are the human connections we make and the wide variety of conversations we have while gardening. I've been engaged in discussions on everything from the state of our industrial food system and processed foods, mental health care provision (or lack thereof), racism, capitalism, celebrities and social media to the state of our local high streets and what to do with tomato gluts.

I intentionally sought out a community garden rather than growing food on an allotment or simply in my own garden at home, which I am privileged enough to have. I notice, however, that quite a few of the people who come here also have allotments, or have had one in the past. Yet they still choose, or end up finding their way, to a community growing space. I'm curious how gardeners often want an allotment and at the same time I'm struck by how many give up their plots or seek to share what's become a burden with friends and family.

Having gardened for quite a few years, some of which has involved growing my own on a tiny scale, I'm aware of how much time and energy is needed and of all the travails that can come with it. Producing these plants can be incredibly satisfying and fulfilling but it can also be demoralising when it doesn't work out – a heart- and back-breaking affair. Sharing the workload and the fruits of those efforts feels much more appealing, rewarding and motivating to me.

One aspect I am particularly sceptical about is the seeming drive in some people to chase an idea of the 'Good Life' with rose-tinted visions of being self-sufficient. I'm interested in querying this notion because I wonder how much of this, alongside the desire to have an allotment, is tied to our dominant culture of individualism. Our society teaches us to value this sense of individualism – our 'own' plot – and to believe that dependency on others is somehow a sign of weakness. We are becoming increasingly isolated in our society, elevating the individual (the consumer – and what we can get and do for ourselves) over the collective (and cultivating reciprocity). This separates us from one another, making us believe that 'I' matter above all else and that we should strive to be self-reliant, to take care of ourselves, to hoard. As Richard Layard says in his book *Can We Be Happier?*, 'We have told our young people that their chief duty is to themselves – to get on.'

While many people seeking the 'Good Life' are envisaging something akin to the famous seventies TV sitcom about a suburban couple pursuing the green dream, it is further fuelled by our social-media-driven age. Floating about in fashionably desirable outfits, gardening influencers post idyllic, idealised photographs of themselves with armfuls of flowers and wooden trugs full of produce from their plots or gardens. The side of social media that encourages self-promotion, competition and consumerism only serves to emphasise this sense of individualism in our society. And so we come to believe the myth that not only is self-sufficiency desirable but that it is even possible.

In the process of buying into these notions, we have a tendency to make invisible all the ways in which we are intimately interdependent, how in fact we rely on our many relationships for survival. We erase how much we depend on each other. This is probably most clearly illustrated through healthcare and food. Both are essential to our lives and well-being and with both we are almost utterly dependent on other people, whether essential workers, care workers, doctors or farmers. Yet these figures are often removed from our everyday view and are chronically undervalued by society. The Nigerian writer, speaker and teacher Bayo Akomolafe talks of noticing how 'our lives are subsidised by the invisible', explaining that until we learn to live alongside and meet the invisible, we shall continue to reproduce the same paradigms that we're trying to escape, be that racism, inequality or climate and biodiversity collapse.

It's worth remembering too that allotments were never intended to allow people to be self-sufficient. In fact they arose out of the opposite impulse. Allotments came into being from the late 1700s into the 1800s after millions of acres of common land had been systematically carved up, enclosed and privatised. They were deliberately designed to keep workers pacified and to ensure that they were *just* happy enough with their lot. There is an argument that the origins of capitalism lay in this enclosure movement in England, when wealthy elites systematically forced people off agricultural and wooded land and denied them access to the resources necessary for survival. Allotments were about control and keeping the working class in line, their aim being to curb anger over land injustices.

Given this backdrop, I certainly don't mean to deny or disparage anyone their desire or right to have their own plot. Most people simply want a relationship with the soil, to be able to produce some of their own food, and to nurture a connection to the natural world. A relationship to land is something so many of us are denied. Today, half the land in England is owned by just one per cent of the population. One in eight households in Britain has no access to a private or shared garden. This rises to more than one in five households in London. It is an intersectional issue too since, in England, black people are nearly four times as likely as white people to have no access to an outdoor space at home, whether that's a private or shared garden, a patio or a balcony.

One afternoon, after a session at the community garden, I go to meet with my friend Maria to chat with her about her allotment. We know each other from the community garden but I'm curious to find out about her relationship with her plot.

When she first took it on five years ago, she didn't have any growing space at home. Now she has a house with a garden and lives within walking distance of the allotment – just two hundred steps away. But the two go together, she tells me, the garden is smaller than the allotment, so they wouldn't be able to transfer what they have on the plot anyway.

The allotment gives her a great deal of joy that she says is difficult to describe. She feels as though she's in her element out there, that time goes by so quickly. I ask if she is able to name the desire that's being satisfied by her visits and she speaks about the need to be in a space where she is on her own with nature. She imagines having conversations with the wildlife she sees there, such as the robin that comes to visit while she digs the earth. For her it's like therapy, 'a spa for my mind', to be in this place where things feel peaceful and in harmony. I can very much relate to all of this. The magic and joy of communing with the more-than-human around us.

Another of my friends from the community garden, Lisa, took on a new plot this summer in her recent retirement. She has a balcony at home but no garden. As Lisa also comes to the community garden to help grow food, I ask her what made her want to get an allotment as well. She laughs. 'I guess because it's mine then, isn't it? It's my fruit and veg, and also I can provide not just stuff for me. I've got two daughters, both married and have kids, [I can] provide some stuff for them as well.

But also my grandsons have come and they've quite enjoyed being on the allotment, doing really simple things.'

My own relationship to gardening and with the earth is a growing, evolving, shifting thing. Just as all relationships are. One of the main ways in which gardening has changed for me during my life is my understanding of what it means to me personally and what it means more broadly – socially and politically. As I've grown more aware of each of these elements, trying to live with greater intention, so my gardening has changed too.

Gardening has always fulfilled a desire. It made me feel good, gave me a sense of peace and serenity. I saw it as a sanctuary away from other people, away from the harshness of the human world. As for Maria, it gave me a connection to nature that felt meaningful. What I didn't understand then was how our dominant culture and our society works to separate humans from the natural world. How humans are so often viewed as superior. I've since come to understand this separation and how it has been constructed. I see how systems of domination can be, and often are, upheld by gardening too. This can manifest in many and various forms, but not least the way we can see certain beings in the garden as 'pests' or 'weeds' and how we might readily seek to destroy, poison, eliminate or tidy with very little consideration for ecosystems or the health of a wider web of life. The way I choose to garden now can be a radical act in disrupting this fabrication.

Today, I see the garden as an ever-changing co-creation between me and all the other animate beings there. It isn't about me controlling and dominating what happens in that space. There's been a shift in my mindset: the lens through which I see a garden is now one of community – a place to practise being in kinship and to cultivate deeper relationships with both my more-than-human and human cousins.

I think this goes some way to explaining why I consciously chose to garden in community when it comes to food growing, rather than putting my name down for my own allotment. There is an element of me seeking the relational aspect of it, the sharing and helping each other – the mutuality of it. In all my conversations with allotmenteer friends, every one of them talked about plot holders swapping produce. I was curious to know whether it went further than this, what sense of community there was on their allotments, if any.

I ask Maria. Does anyone share labour or work? She hasn't seen that, she replies; people just stick to their plots. I ask if there is a committee or any discussion of how to manage or run the place. The answer is, no, not really, apart from an annual meeting and AGM. But then, towards the end of our conversation, I ask a final question about diversity on the site. There is a Nepalese community, she tells me. They do things in a very different way, grow in a different way too, sticking to just a few crops. There are around ten families. Then Maria remembers my much earlier question: 'They work as a family,' she tells me, 'and they do help each other.'

I ask her how growing on the allotment compares to her experience of growing at the community garden. The latter was completely different, she says, because she was having conversations there, learning from someone else, sharing recipes, sharing tips. On the plot it's just her; everyone is very focused on their own growing. 'There is something that happens on the allotment,' she explains. 'There's a sense of urgency that if I go to the allotment it's because there is something that I need to do.'

Another friend of mine, Hollie, who is British Chinese like myself, has wanted an allotment since she was nineteen. She was finally allocated one in her London borough of Newham in 2021, having been on the waiting list for seven years. Before this, she had been on a ten-year waiting list in Brixton until she moved out of the borough. She has a keen interest in growing – food especially. Her grandparents had a big garden and she grew up watching them tend Chinese vegetables. Part of her wanted to copy them. 'These experiences can be really formative in your life,' she explains, 'and you might not know why you want to do something but it's been imprinted on you.'

Her plot is on the main path so she, her husband and their baby pass a lot of people and people pass them too. On a Sunday they will spend a couple of hours there and chat to neighbours. She particularly enjoys that there are quite a few East and Southeast Asian allotmenteers there, which she finds comforting: 'It's easy to see someone who looks like you, from a similar culture, and bond on that level and on the fact that they also have an allotment,' she says. The vegetables shared can sometimes be a perk too, saving her a trip to the Chinese supermarket. The other day someone gave her a bitter melon. There are also lots of South Asian and Eastern European people at the site, which means when produce is shared it's varied and interesting. Hollie is given different vegetables and seeds that she might not find in the shops, for example Bulgarian and Lithuanian types of tomatoes that people have brought back from home – a joy of being in a diverse borough and a diverse space.

Like Maria, she finds it really satisfying to be at the plot. More satisfying than she finds her own garden. She wonders whether she finds it a more inspiring space to grow because everyone else is doing it and inspiration comes from watching. 'There's an element of competition when you go to the allotment,' she muses. 'As you're passing other people's plots you compare your own growing efforts to others.'

The site Hollie is on has recently gone back into council control and a committee has been elected for the first time in five years. Management of the site had been pretty poor up until now, she tells me. The community aspect of having and tending an allotment is a big draw for Hollie and something she would really like to get involved in a lot more. 'Do you feel like there is currently a community?' I ask her. 'No . . . um, only in that I see the same people every time I go,' she says. 'There's not much organising?' I venture. 'Exactly, I'd like more organised fun. Maybe having get-togethers. Currently that doesn't exist.'

Unlike the council-run sites that Hollie and Maria have plots on, Lisa's is on a privately managed site with facilities that seem a lot more substantial and with more investment. There is a large shed with tea- and coffee-making facilities, drinks in the fridge, and a microwave so you can warm your soup up in the winter. There's a toilet on site. In the winter there are regular coffee mornings and various other gatherings throughout the year, including an annual show in the summer, a quiz night and a fish-and-chip supper. 'They are trying to bring people together and make it more of a community,' Lisa tells me. The site has a committee, an AGM and there are also trustees.

I ask Lisa if she often sees other people on her visits to her allotment. 'Not as many as I thought I would . . . There are over a hundred plots there so it's a big site. But I only ever see maybe four or five people maximum and they're all dotted around the other plots, so when you're walking around you might see there's somebody over there, or over there. It's never been busy when I've been there, even on a weekend. It surprises me because all of the plots are very well looked after. But I suppose I'm only going two or three times a week, maybe for an hour or two. There are so many other times that people could go.' 'Have you started recognising people at all?' I ask. 'No, not really. I did meet the woman on the plot next to me and we had a chat a few weeks ago, but I've not seen her there since. And then the people behind me, they were an older couple and they popped round when I was there one day and gave me some cooking apples and cucumbers, so there's quite a lot of sharing of produce goes on, but I've just found out that they're giving up their plot so it's becoming vacant.'

When we talk about community, what do we really mean? And if it exists, is it built on strong foundations? These conversations brought to mind something I recall hearing from Minna Salami, the Nigerian-Finnish and Swedish feminist author and social critic: that community is about relationship rather than simply about 'togetherness'. You can be together in one place, but not have healthy or thriving relationships – a real community. This is as true on a community garden as it is on an allotment.

In a world where there is so much separation, dispossession and individualism, where we are increasingly pushed to extremes, into tribes and echo chambers, building community and strengthening relationships through growing seems an opportunity for us to find common ground. Can community gardens and allotments be sites of possible resistance, places where we might build different kinds of relationships and understanding? Absolutely.

In his book *How to Resist: Turn Protest to Power*, Matthew Bolton – Director at Citizens UK – writes how it's in collective action and local associations that people learn to lead, to listen, to cooperate and to compromise. Such fundamental skills and attitudes underpin a democratic society. He points out that local places where people come together regularly with a positive purpose have the potential to be engines of democratic participation over the coming decades.

Yet I can't help but feel that recent seismic events both nationally and globally, from Brexit to Black Lives Matter to ongoing conflicts in the Middle East, have been rocking our relational foundations, our values, our sense of reciprocity, and exposing them to be pretty shaky at best. Being in community doesn't just happen. It requires effort, attention and intention. It requires tending. It needs action. We have to want to advocate, to build mutual relationships and skills, to exchange resources and to have open conversations in which we truly listen.

People gathering in community gardens or allotments – from different political and social backgrounds, from different countries and with different outlooks – often have common interests that have brought them there in the first place. There is so much potential to be relational in these places, to practise these new ways of being. It could be such a potent thing, growing community while nurturing plants that sustain us, growing power over a shared joy in food, growing our connection to the earth and to each other, prioritising access to land, human health and the health of the wider ecosystems of which we're a part.

Tony Scott, Newburn allotments

PEACEABLE KINGDOMS

Graeme Rigby

These three pieces are from *Peaceable Kingdoms*, a book I made with photographer Peter Fryer, published in 1992 by Newcastle upon Tyne's Leisure Services Department. The whole project was a joy. I'd collaborated with Peter on an earlier documentary project and we liked working together. He'd been commissioned to document allotments in Newcastle and persuaded the council the work should end up as a book and that they should commission me to write it. He'd already been working on the project for several months and the allotment holders liked him and trusted him. He took me round the different gardens where he'd been taking photographs and, if I was a friend of his, they were all fine with it.

As a writer working with oral testimony, you need people to open up – not because you want to know the secrets of their lives, but because there's a quality in their voices when they feel able to become their own storytellers. It's a generalisation, but however authentic the voice, middle-class interviewees tend to qualify any statements they make into non-existence. There's something special about allotments, however. In their own gardens, allotment holders seem to feel secure. The gardens, the vegetables and flowers, the pigeons and the poultry, the sheds, crees and makeshift structures are all extensions of their own personalities. The interviewees for *Peaceable Kingdoms* generously gave me their time and opened up without prompting: the respite it offered from a partner's cancer, the space it gave that made a relationship possible, the delight in the detailed beauty of a flower, nights spent watching by a car-battery-powered light as seeds flipped over or the spiralling growth of your seedling leeks.

The words here are all theirs. I edited only to give shape and reveal, if I could, the beauty I found in what they had told me. There was a lovely man who talked about preparing chrysanthemum blooms for competitions: I could only aspire to doing something as delicate and precise. It was over thirty years ago and the time I spent with each of them – and with Peter – is imprinted in my mind as a kind of idyll: one of the two best writing gigs of my life (Bombay duck fishermen in Arnala gave me the other).

Etal Park: A Community of Men Talking

DICK ROBSON: It was 1978, it started. We had a meeting with the council. What happened was, there was eighty names for thirty-five gardens, so we had to put it all in the hat and draw them out. We got thirty-five names out and from them we formed a committee. We had nothing: there was just a bare field, really. It took us about two years to get every allotment taken, because people were coming, taking them on, then they found it was hard work. We used to go around at nights, knocking doors and say, 'Oh, there's an allotment there, you know.' Then we started ruling, if you didn't dig your allotment within a certain time, you were out. It's surprising how many people did lose their gardens through that. Eventually we got organised, but there were no huts or anything like that.

TOMMY TAZEY: The council wanted every potting shed and greenhouse the same. That was taking the individual char-acter away from the plot holder, to me. As long as your hut is respectable and tidy and it's not an eyesore, corrugated iron and all that, it should be all right . . . Everything uniform, it'd just break your heart.

DICK ROBSON: The council wouldn't allow anything with there being houses all around. They said the huts had to be uni-form and for us to buy the building from the council, but we said, 'No way!' Since then, it's built up and built up. We had to put our own water in; dig our own ditches for our water; put our own taps in. We put our own clinker in for the paths. Since then, you'll find a lot have put concrete paths in or flagstones. But the gardens have taken off now, really well. They've had to, because of the housing round, because if they're an eyesore we'll lose them, they'll take them away from us. So we have to be very careful. It's a great thing, being able to have an allotment: it's being outside . . .

JOHN SMITH: It's something to do instead of sitting in the house like an invalid all the time. When you first come into it, naturally, you've just had, mebbes, a little house garden, a few flowers; you don't know nothing about veg. Then you start to get interested and you get talking to people. They'll say, 'Try this plant . . . Try that plant.' I think the main thing is the community of men, talking.

DICK ROBSON: Everybody helps each other. If I haven't got my sprouts, I say, 'Have you any sprouts?' They'll say, 'Jimmy might have some . . . John might have some . . .' And you go and ask and they say, 'Oh, got a few.' It's real good companionship.

JIM BRECKONS: You get a lot of lads, who aren't even on the allotment and they come across in the car and they say, 'I've just had PVC windows in and there's nowt the matter with the old frames and glass. If I dump them down, will you take them?' You build up your greenhouses with them.

TOMMY TAZEY: Saves a lot of money.

DICK ROBSON: I remember John Marshall: he worked on the buildings and he brought a great wagon, a dumper, a great, big, massive load of rough sand and he tipped it over there, and we used to sell sand at twenty pence a barrow load. That's how we got the sand in here . . . It's all stuff that's given away.

JOHN SMITH: You get stuff taken 'n' all.

DICK ROBSON: You do get some trouble here, but compared to some, we don't get a lot of vandalism. We get kids that come in and they'll break into a hut and take nothing.

TOMMY TAZEY: They turn the taps on and then the taps is on all night.

JIM BRECKONS: We seem to have spasms. Odd times they'll come and they'll bust every door open and they'll lay all your gear outside. The next time, three or four months later, they'll come again and they'll break everything. They took all these turnips out, one time, and they put all the turnip tops back in. Of course, one day, the lad comes in: 'What the hell's the matter with them turnips?' He looked and he found there was nothing at the bottom.

JOHN SMITH: There was a woman in one of the houses, over there. She had getten up, for some reason, in the middle of the night. As she couldn't sleep, she thought, 'Oh, I'll make meself a cup of tea . . .' And she seen a bloke digging potatoes out, with a light, in the middle of the night: pinched five rows of potatoes.

DICK ROBSON: We had one lad, used to break in and he'd leave a note: 'Seek and Destroy.' He used to put a note down with a brick on it, in whatever garden he'd broken into. 'Seek and Destroy.'

TOMMY TAZEY: Aye. 'You have been visited by SAD.' You'd go: 'Sad?' Then, all of a sudden, the next note we got was: 'You don't know who SAD is, but it means Seek and Destroy.'

DICK ROBSON: We've had break-ins where they've taken things. I had a camping-gas burner and a bottle that was taken. They've taken spades and tools, things like that.

JIM BRECKONS: There was the day the Hoe and Rake got one . . . We had this pub, when we did the home brew. The sign's still there: The Hoe and Rake. We used to sit in there, it was like a bus, six seats on either side. Come in one night, there was five gallons bottled and ready to drink and five gallon on the brew and there wasn't one drop left. Someone had pinched the bloody lot.

DICK ROBSON: We've got a shop. It started in here, but it wasn't very satisfactory, because it wasn't very secure. The council helped at that particular time. There was some training scheme, where they built these things out of really good timber. I went to ask if we could get one. They said we couldn't have one, but they would fund the money if we could build one ourselves. So I told the lads and they decided to build one. We got a grant and we bought the bricks and then we found we needed more money, so we asked for another grant. We got three or four grants, altogether, and we built a hut that's secure. It's not only for the members. Members of the community can also use the shop. We sell peat, Gro-bags, fertiliser – all kinds of fertiliser, paraffin, fish food, canes, seeds, phosphagen . . . All the things that's required on an allotment. There's a rotavator you can hire . . .

JOHN SMITH: This hut we're in now, all the allotment holders can use it. It's there for them if they want it. A lot of them have got their own places now, where they make their own tea, this, that and the other. But it used to be, each man'd hoy fifty pence a time in, so we used to go round the abattoirs, come back: sausage, bacon, savouries, ham shanks . . . In the winter, there was always broth on, sausage sandwiches. You got a lot for your fifty pence a week. Well, it used to last them four days, that . . . We don't do it now. People seem to be going individual. There's a little animosity creeps in . . .

JIM BRECKONS: Some wouldn't pay their fifty pences.

JOHN SMITH: We still hoy money into the box, to make our tea, but we've more or less stopped the cooking.

DICK ROBSON: It's the same crowd that comes in, like, but it's there for anyone. I'll be working down the garden and they come to the door and shout, 'Tea's up!' And I'll come and get a cup of tea, so it's ideal.

TOMMY TAZEY: We had dumplings and ham shanks. We used to bring loaves of bread and just dive in.

JOHN SMITH: (*brandishing a large pan*) Well, we did cook some very big ones, like . . .

TOMMY TAZEY: Then, we'd finish off with the home brew . . .

JOHN SMITH: We just used to gan and buy the ham shanks over at the abattoir in Gateshead. Somebody would hoy a couple of swedes in. Somebody would hoy carrots in. Owt.

DICK ROBSON: It was good stuff 'n' all.

JIM BRECKONS: They were real rib-claggers . . .

Nuns Moor: A Quiet Little Allotment
Margaret Dryland

My father had a huge garden and many a lovely day I spent just lying in the grass, looking at the sky. One day, I was lying, looking up into the blue sky and I was thinking, 'Heaven's just above there.' I gave myself such a fright. I was terrified to think that there was a heaven. I didn't want to go to heaven.

Well, that's how it started. I was always keen on digging and things like that. I learned most of what I know about gardening from me father. He wouldn't let us touch the garden, but we could stand and admire and just think about it. And I remember when me father had to give the garden up and the house – it was condemned – he got an allotment and I said I would come down and I would help him. Now, I was pregnant at the time. My husband was in the army. I was just digging things up galore. 'Well, we don't really need this . . .' and out it would come. My father didn't say, 'No, leave it, it's good.' When I look back now, I feel so ashamed of myself.

When my husband got the allotment I sometimes used to go down with him, but he wouldn't let me do anything.

And yet I loved gardening. When we first came up here and got this house in 1948, I thought it was marvellous, putting lettuces in and things like that. It was really great, but I knew then, he didn't want me in the garden. He must have thought gardening was heavy work and it's for a man, not for a woman, because he used to say, 'Oh, don't bother to come in. I'll do this.' I thought, 'Well, that's probably the way men are, and you cannot go above them, can you?' And I thought, 'Well, I've got enough to do in the house and I've got the children to see to, so if he wants to do the garden, let him get on with it.'

I used to go down the allotment with him, but I'm a great reader: I can read anywhere, anytime. So I used to take a flask and everything and I would say, 'Is there anything I can do? I could pull some weeds up . . .' And I could do everything he was doing, but I'm not going to shove me nose in where it's not wanted. 'No,' he says. 'It's all right.'

Yet, we used to go on fishing holidays and he was always saying, 'Oh man, don't sit reading. Come here: I've got ump-teen rods. I'll put one in for you.' 'No,' I says. 'I don't want to fish.' So at the finish, I said, 'All right, give us a rod.' And as soon as I caught a fish I was hooked. I've never stopped loving fish after that. I would do anything that I wanted to do, but I didn't want to do fishing until he practically made me.

When my husband died, he told me to give the allotment up. I said, 'Yes, well . . .' And then I thought, 'Why should I?'

I wanted to get out of the house. I wanted to be quiet and on me own, so I went down to the allotment. Of course, it was covered in weeds, by that time, but I said to the secretary, 'I think I'll just keep the allotment going.' I said, 'It's terrible with the weeds, but I'll just do me best.'

I think it's something born in you really. You've got to have a feeling for nature. That's definitely the way of it. It's all right, a tough man saying, 'I'll go and sow an allotment.' But some of them can't do it. They'll say, 'I've got a bad back.' Rubbish. I've had a bad back for years and it's never stopped me. I keep saying, 'My God, I'll have to stop this.' But I'll sit down and have a rest for five minutes. If you're interested in anything, it'll never stop you.

That was three years ago, come October, my husband died, but next year they take that garden off me, because they're going to put a road over the Moor again. Another road. That Town Moor was a beautiful moor, but now everybody's getting chunks of it, just spiriting it away. That's the way they do it.

I hadn't been there very long when I found out. I just couldn't believe it. I thought, 'No, that'll never happen . . .' So I went to a couple of chaps that are on the committee and I said, 'Is it true?' They said, 'Yes.' And I said, 'But why should I lose mine?' He said, 'Yours is going to be the one that's going to get covered in concrete.' I said, 'What's it for?' And it was coming from the Redheugh Bridge through the town. The first route was supposed to be where the golf course is, but they weren't going to allow anybody to snatch a bit of their course, so it fell back on us.

They offered me another garden, but what a state it was in: you've never see anything like it in your life. It had some beautiful leeks and things, but they had never, ever tidied up the stones and I thought, 'How the hell can I shift them? I'm only a woman on me own.' And there was a great water tank, you know. And it didn't have the privacy. It's a quiet little allotment, the one I've got. It's lovely. I really like it. So I told them, 'No.' I didn't want the other one.

It's funny. You see, when these things happen to me, I can curse and swear about it and then I'll say, 'Eee, well, you expected this, didn't you . . .' And I'll just laugh to meself for assuming why I should be singled out. No. I just get on with my life and you've got to be tough to face up to different things.

I know I'll miss it.

Newburn: A Little Bit Kingdom
Tony Scott

Any depressions that you might have, they just physically go within minutes of you getting down here and sitting down.

I think you're just away from the home environment – not that we don't get on at home, but it's a fact that it's nice to be able to come away, if you want to come away, and have your own little bit kingdom. This is my little bit kingdom.

I've got me cooker, that's a Calor gas fridge there, a sink unit, TV and I've got me stereo system under there. I don't use the turntable because of the dust and that, but it plays the tapes great. They're all things that I've picked up for nothing. The lights is in. I've got a generator, which I run my garden off and I run the lad's next door, as well. I've run a cable right down the bottom to Ray Blackburn's garden, for a water pump for him, because he's got plenty of water in his garden, but he's got to hump it from the bottom to the top.

I've got a massive well under here, beneath this, which is a trapdoor. It holds something like two thousand gallons of water. I'm fairly handy. I work for the Gas Board. I'm a service technician: in that sort of work, you pick up lots of crafts. But all this has cost basically nothing to build. It's all scrap timber and bits of glass that I've picked up.

I probably spend more time down here than what I do in the house, if truth were known, especially over the last fifteen weeks, because I've been on the sick. I'm waiting to go into hospital. I've got a blocked, or a semi-blocked artery in the neck and it's giving me blackouts. So I'm down here all the time. And the kids are down here: soon as they finish school, they're straight down here, that sort of thing. They divvent bother going home. They have their teas here. They're here till sometimes ten o'clock at night, especially when they're off school.

When you finish work, you like to relax. There's nothing worse than sitting and the telephone goes. You're up and down off your seat all the time. Here, you can do a little bit of enjoyment, you can do a little bit of weeding, planting, anything you wish. Come back and sit in here, five minutes, pot of tea, everything disappears. The kids are the same. There's always something for them to do: clean the hen run, doing the chickens, collecting the eggs, doing the weeding . . .

I get five, six, seven, eight, ten kids down here on a Sunday. They all get involved. If I say, 'Right, I want that patch weeding', there'll be five or six of them actually in amongst the cabbages, pulling the weeds. They know exactly where to put them. If I tell them to put them on the heap, they put them on there: the likes of nettles, thistles, that sort of thing. They've all got their gloves down here. But if it's chickweed, they automatically just take it into the run for the hens.

It teaches the kids a lot. It teaches them self-respect, how to use tools, machinery, that sort of thing, because I do teach them. I wouldn't just leave them to get on with it. It also lets them see things that they would never see: frogs, newts, diseases in your garden and stuff, potato blight. They do pick up that kind of thing. My leek was bending over the other day and the laddie, it's only what he's picked up and he's heard off different people: 'Is that *Botrytis* or that rot stuff, Fusarium rot?' And he has got it. When a kid takes an interest in something like that, there's always something you can build on. To me, there is, anyway.

FROM SWEET PEAS
TO POLITICS

Sara Venn

Growing food has been the constant throughout my life. Brought up in the seventies by parents I now realise were looking at alternative lifestyles that circumnavigated the capitalist norm, the allotment at the bottom of our long and skinny garden was impressive. It was where I ate my first pea straight from the pod and found the miracle of the soft cocoon of the broad bean pod. And it was the first place I learned the miracle of a seed becoming something delicious that I could eat.

While many others played at the 'Good Life', my parents lived it – along with our neighbours who effectively ran a smallholding with chickens and the occasional pig, which, I think, we shared.

On leaving that house at around seven or eight, a new home meant a significantly smaller garden. And so it was that my parents rented their first 'proper' allotment and I was enthralled. For a start, the entire site was made up of people like our old neighbours, minus the pigs. What I failed to realise at the time was that in the mid- to late seventies the allotment world was a patriarchal society and that women on site were rare. My mum was one of them. I recall her frustration when one old boy or another commented that 'allotments aren't women's work' or asked where her husband was, but eventually they got used to her and what they jokingly called her 'Northern ways'.

That allotment fed our family. It fed friends and neighbours and throughout the miners' strikes it was the source of the main ingredients for the food parcels we took up to the striking communities. It fed us at the peace camps we visited at Greenham Common. It taught me that food and community were interlinked, and that while we were all pretty different on those plots, there was something about allotment life that brought people together, if only to bemoan slug attacks.

It was a place of refuge from the hideous eighties world of money and Thatcherism and as it taught me about soil, food growing and nature, it also taught me that food and growing are deeply political. It made me learn about the enclosures, drew me to research the many movements that have fought for access to land throughout this island's history. It also made me realise that activism is about action and that while there is a place for protest, which I have never been afraid to join, the simple act of growing and bringing food to the community is one whose power should never be doubted.

Most of all, it taught me who I am. That however much I thought I could fight the pull, in the end I would always return to the land, eventually making it my career as well as my life. Yet little did I realise the effect this would have when over four decades later I had the idea of Edible Bristol, an organisation that I have now run for ten years and that is based in food and land justice, supporting communities to grow food on unproductive and often public land. Food is the one thing that unites us. Growing and cooking with one another offers support to those with whom we might otherwise struggle to find common ground. It brings us together when there is so much that might otherwise divide us.

In the mid-nineties, in my mid-twenties and having had a turbulent few years, I began working in horticulture, taking courses, exams, gaining qualifications. While my parents had moved away from our beloved allotment site, and as a young mum I had also had to put growing to one side, it was now becoming increasingly obvious that I needed a space to put what I was learning in theory into action. Yet we were living in a small housing association flat, with no garden other than a small border at the front of the building, which I fought to manage while the landlord insisted on a contractor. So an allotment it was. Not just any allotment, however, but one on the same site as my parents' old plot, a short distance away. Immediately it felt like home. A place to experiment, to feed my own family, to escape the increasingly capitalist world and to return to what felt important. What I hadn't expected was to return to the same attitude to women on the site.

Historically women have always picked up men's work during difficult times, including during both world wars. From the Land Girls to the Dig for Victory campaigns, we see women working the land, growing food and feeding communities, so by the nineties I had expected to see some change from the patriarchal nonsense my mum had put up with. But no. To my absolute amazement, those very same questions were being flung my way. My then boyfriend and now husband was regularly berated by those men for 'allowing' me to do all the work. Alongside these comments, though, were others that bothered me more.

Over my entire growing career I have fought not to use any form of pesticides. When I began my career, pesticide use was absolutely the norm and continues to be for so many growers. With this comes the need to become a qualified sprayer, a role that I loathed and avoided as often as I could despite holding several different types of licence for my work. The first thing my first spraying tutor taught our cohort was that before considering pesticides we should think about the techniques that you could use instead of chemical intervention. That stuck with me and, time and again, the team on the nursery and I proved that alternative actions worked just as well. Instead of spending our days killing 'pests', we could concentrate on helping the plants thrive, and with it create a healthy ecosystem that meant that the amount of pest and disease was negligible anyway. Eventually the nursery stopped all spraying and chemical fertiliser, and productivity increased over our four acres. The right plant in the right place, correct watering, mulching, efficient movement of plants through the system – all of this grows better plant stock than continuously fighting against nature's otherwise out-of-sync web. Here nature bloomed and led the way.

My allotment allowed me to focus on growing with nature long before I had heard the term agroecology, and rely on permaculture processes learned long ago when gardening with mum, our neighbours and even my granny. I was working with the land and a part of that for me has always been supporting soil health and biodiversity.

So imagine the horror when an allotment neighbour sprayed a quarter of my plot with glyphosate right at the start of my lease. When I asked why he had done this without my permission, he replied he was doing me a favour. 'You don't want that weed getting out of control,' he said, refusing to listen when I said it was a green manure, feeding the soil. To him that was nothing but 'hippy nonsense'. Imagine the horror when I was berated for not digging, told that compost mulches would only be a haven for weeds, and that no one hoed any more.

At one point even my compost bays were questioned. There was one huge heap in the car park that was communal but regularly full of couch grass with roots and willow herb with seeds, so I had made my own three-bay system. Hardly controversial, you'd think, but apparently it was going to bring rats to my plot. It was around this time that I undertook the Garden Organic Master Composter training, and was able to use this to persuade the committee that since I was regularly turning my compost, it was far more likely that Ratty and his family and friends were living in the communal heap. The committee acquiesced but there were still mumblings about the mad hippy in the corner plot.

Now, I say 'mad hippy' not to stereotype myself or anyone else trying to embrace nature, but because this was genuinely a phrase that people used, and sometimes to my face. This was a time in the nineties when lad culture was at its height and young people, let alone young women, were not expected to be growing thriving allotments. I took my number down and replaced it with a sign saying 'Hippy Central'. I refused to be othered; classic divisionary tactics ignored.

While all this rhetoric continued, I turned what had been an unloved plot into one that was not only beautiful and productive but that also worked alongside nature. From the herb garden at the front through mulched beds full of annual veg to the more permanent planting at the far end, what no one could deny was that this crazy woman was growing a plot that was feeding not just her family, but filling freezers of friends, becoming a circular system that fed itself. Not only did I have a compost system that was returning the garden's own waste to the ground to feed its soil, but comfrey patches and a nettle patch provided feeds, as well as raised eyebrows: 'Aren't they weeds?' Allowing some veg to go to flower, alongside edible flowers and flowering herbs, meant the plot was buzzing with pollinators too.

Of course, everything that I was doing here on the allotment was setting me up truly to understand the importance of ecosystems and why nature's health is inherently allied to ours. These were the days before we understood about biodiversity breakdown, and to many of my fellow allotment holders bugs were just something to get rid of any way you could. However, you had only to watch the sparrows that lived in the hedge next to the plot flying to the roses and dahlias, gently picking the aphids off and flying to their nests where their young tucked into them as a feast, to see that everything is a part of the circle of life. It's only when you disrupt that that things go awry.

I was often asked what I did as a job and there were frequent looks of surprise; assumptions that I worked in a garden centre on the tills or in a clean sales job. And once again the comments returned were all too familiar. 'Isn't that men's work?' 'I bet you struggle to keep up . . .' There was even one person who inferred my role must be making tea and sweeping. Yet while all this was going on, more women were beginning to appear on site, growing beautiful gardens that were as productive as any traditional plot. Slowly, a community of new allotmenteers was coming into being.

Now, of course there were identifiable reasons for this. Hugh Fearnley-Whittingstall's 'River Cottage' series had first aired in 1999 and interest in foraging and food growing was increasing. The financial crash of 2008 saw the Incredible Edible movement gain favour and, in the US, stories from Detroit and other cities began to appear, where community food growing was stopping people going hungry and creating livelihoods, just as it had in Cuba. The Slow Food movement, focused on local food, was gaining momentum alongside La Via Campesina, both raising knowledge about who really feeds populations across the globe.

People suddenly realised that they wanted to know where their food came from, who grew it, and most importantly how. Awareness of the effects of pesticides not only on people but also on our land was growing, and while organic products began to become available in supermarkets, slowly the rise of community-supported agriculture, veg boxes and local organic shops began.

Food felt as if it was becoming political. Or perhaps I was waking up fully to the politics of food and land.

In 2013, I left my old home and with it the allotment to take up a new role in a nursery near Bristol. Saying farewell to that site, not knowing whether I'd be able to access a new plot in a new city, was hard. I knew I wouldn't have a garden, so I put myself on the closest allotment waiting list and got involved in a local project in the meantime. I grew flowers on the community site, and chatted with so many people as I was doing so, giving the flowers away. A five-minute walk from Bristol's main shopping area, it was a place of such cultural diversity that just by being there I felt I was soaking in new knowledge every day.

But I missed growing food. I missed the community that gave me the sense of purpose I felt stewarding that piece of land. So eventually I rang the allotment office. I told them I didn't care where in the city it was, but that I'd pretty much do anything to find a plot. I had no idea what I was stepping into.

Stapleton Allotment site is on Bristol's Blue Finger, the city's historic market garden. Called the Blue Finger because on agricultural maps this farmland is shown as a deep blue, its soil is grade A1, the best medium for growing we have in the UK. Only 3 per cent of British land is of this quality. Not only does it hold water in drought, but its structure allows it to mitigate flooding. When I arrived on site to see the plot they had for me, with a greenhouse and a shed, I was smitten.

I'd noticed a sign on the gates saying 'Save the Allotments' and a small amount of chatting with the reps on site told me that there was change coming, but at that point my naivety took hold and I honestly believed that no one could be so ridiculous as to lose allotments for a road. So I began. I made beds, I mulched, planted perennial shrubs and climbers, created a new compost system, grew greenhouse crops, planted the quince I'd brought with me from the south-east, along with various other containers that had travelled with me from that tiny garden at the front of our flat. I spent hours, days, whole weekends creating a garden that was filled with colour, scents, fruit, veg and where I could once again experiment not just with growing techniques but with this extraordinary soil in which everything flourished. That first year in Bristol was tough, but the allotment gave me a place where I could hide and on which I could play. I got to know folk on site, made pals, drank tea, and grew anything and everything. I imagined I'd be growing here forever.

At the beginning of 2014, I set about creating Edible Bristol, the organisation I continue to run, which supports community-led food growing on under-used land across the city. When there is so much of this kind of space in an urban landscape, it always seemed ridiculous to me that urban food growing is so often done behind gates and fences, immediately making it inaccessible to most.

Growing food in new community gardens where divides can be mended, where the horrors of both climate and social injustice can be discussed and understood in a safe space, is – of course – intensely political. Yet the one thing that surprised me was that suddenly people wanted my opinions and feelings on a multitude of linked subjects, from growing to land access and local production. In all of this, I was slung onto a public platform that, while an absolute privilege, also threw my mental health into crisis, making me feel like an impostor.

Over the last decade, levels of poverty have increased exponentially, and what was set up as an organisation to support food growing has now become one that supports communities to feed those in their neighbourhoods that are most vulnerable, helping food aid projects across the city. What some might see as a load of folk engaging in guerrilla-type gardening is in reality a cohort of radical food-growing groups fighting for both social and environmental justice.

But why am I telling you all this?

Because the allotment became my sanctuary. It had no expectations. While I navigated working with the council, local organisations, MPs, landowners and lots of other amazing people, on the allotment I could process the busy happenings of the previous day. Mulching beds, sowing seeds and planting out crops allowed me to work through issues, to find solutions while being productive on this precious land that just kept giving. But, more than this, it became my safe space at a time when our housing situation was far from stable. Our landlady was having some serious mental health issues that were affecting all her tenants, and the allotment was the only place where I could be guaranteed security and calm. Feeding people from my plot, my family, friends and neighbours, is a part of who I am. It gave me that back.

For renters, allotments allow a freedom to experiment and a sense of ownership of land when the majority of landlords and letting agents at the best discourage and at the worst ban growing entirely. I once lost half my deposit for planting things in empty beds because they would need removing before the next tenants moved in. I've had letting agents roll their eyes at my job and forcibly point out that gardening is not allowed. In one place I was seen as such a risk that we were refused a tenancy because the square of concrete with a washing line out the back was 'not to be used for gardening purposes'. Land is instead often 'managed' by contractors whose main aim is to keep paths clear of any plant life, and keep areas tidy. Their weapons of choice are strimmers, brush cutters and chemical weed control, and their choice of plants are what, in the trade, we jokingly call 'car park planting'. Plants that need minimum maintenance, that will cope with virtually anything and that are no threat to humans: hebes, cotoneaster, euonymus, juniper. Allotments offer a possibility that is otherwise lacking in so many lives.

Of course, renters are often young people, and while we do often hear young people aren't interested in food growing, the reality is many are but they cannot access land even to begin. The rise in interest in houseplants and the rise in people house sharing well into their thirties is no surprise.

But back to my plot. In 2015 my little world collapsed as the local council decided they were going to 'reimagine' the site, decimating a large area of trees where a huge amount of nature thrived so that a bus lane could be added. The allotment site was in uproar, divided as always in these situations into those who were effectively saying, 'over my dead body', and those who thought they might be in for some kind of windfall. I don't think I need to tell you which side I stood on. We wrote letters, we lobbied councillors, went to planning committees, but finally – despite enormous effort – planning permission was granted. At that stage Bristol's environmental activists rallied and within days people were living in the trees to try to save them. There was twenty-four-hour security on the allotment gates, and a twenty-four-hour campsite under the trees where the kettle was always on and where

Rising Up, the first iteration of Extinction Rebellion, seemed to grow from the soil and the roots. The site I loved felt as though it was disappearing. I joined the protest, we marched, we lobbied the mayor, wrote more letters and appeared on local and national news. We held the land for eighteen days and while effectively nothing changed, those precious soils of Bristol's Blue Finger crawling beside both sides of the M32 were raised in the consciousness of the city and beyond.

While technically no plots were lost, a third of the site was moved onto land that had never been used as allotments before. This land was weed ridden and, by the time it had been set into allotment plots, had been compacted by machinery building the road, dripping diesel onto the soil as they went. Gardeners who had worked the land for literally generations, with one lady losing the plot her family had been working since the thirties, felt they were being expected to start all over and their grief was palpable.

During this time, the site changed in other ways too. Round-the-clock security meant we had to show a letter from the council to access our plots. Welded mesh fencing surrounding the camp and the allotment site had been erected, cars were checked in case they contained protesters, and the security patrolled with huge dogs that they often let roam despite complaints. Anyone seen to be moving between the allotment site and the campsite was treated with caution and no one other than allotment tenants could access the plots. The days of friends gathering, tea parties in sheds, bringing folk along who might have needed a quiet space were gone. And with it the camaraderie on site melted away. Some people decided they wouldn't be coming back until it was all over, others like me stayed and tried to carry on, supporting the folk who were losing their plots. But it was hard to concentrate or to feel engaged in growing in the chaos.

Eventually the trees were lost, the camp disbanded and while the security remained a while, in theory plot life should have just carried on. But there was a change I hadn't expected. The fight had not just split the site; my brain too felt cleft. I couldn't be there without becoming distraught and distracted by the chainsaws on the trees, by the loss of birdsong and the sound of leaves in the breeze. The soul of the site was gone, and with it my sanctuary. I was grieving.

At the same time, our insecure housing situation was coming to a head, and with a heavy heart I came to the decision that since we were moving to a different area of the city, I would give up my plot. By now, I knew the folk at the allotment office and they kindly agreed that as soon as we were settled they'd find me somewhere new. And so I began again. Here was a site in South Bristol that looked out over the entire city, where balloons were seen traversing the sky and where people were kind, and no one was likely to run a road through. The plot hardly needed any work and so I could just get on with growing while healing from the traumas of the last site. However, though we had moved from insecure housing to slightly less insecure housing, it was into an area deeply troubled by inequality, and for two years my mental health wavered. Despite the plot's beautiful outlook and wonderful gardeners, the magic just wasn't there and when we moved again two years later, it was almost with relief that I gave the plot back.

Nowadays I manage a large, three-plot site where Edible Bristol runs courses and workshops, and where the food goes to volunteers and into the local communities through various organisations. Yet I realise, as I sit here writing this surrounded by these plots, that though I love them I'm very keen not to hold any personal ownership of them. And I wonder if that is my way of keeping myself safe from the grief of any further loss. We tie so much of ourselves to the soil.

When it comes to my home, I'm still a renter and as I get older, and I'm five decades away from the first plot my parents leased, I realise that in this modern age of assumed home ownership for all, the insecurity of being a renter and therefore a gardener without a garden of my own will never leave me. In the last two places we've rented, our landlords have been keen for me to use the garden fully, making it easier to utilise the space outside the back door. Yet there's a boggling doubt always there. And I know I'm not alone, especially in a world where landlords can kick you out at a moment's notice, as happened to us during the second Covid lockdown. On being told the news, my immediate reaction was: 'But my garden . . .' And so I guess my feelings about this garden are similar to those about my second Bristol allotment. It's hard to take true ownership of something that you feel could disappear at any moment. But of course that's not a reason not to try again, is it?

So I'll leave you in the knowledge that I've applied for a new allotment site, in my new area of south-west Wales, and the cycle turns again . . .

THIS ALLOTMENT

Rob Cowen

The gate would not open: deadlock.
Key stuck firmly in padlock. And me,
harried, struggling, until I was ready
to abandon the whole damn thing
before it had begun. An intervention:
someone passing with the right tools
said: *'Don't fret. This happens a lot.*
You just need to know the knack.'
Hands twisted with experience,
then, just like that, I was through.
Carrying all I had. Arriving in a new place.
Searching for a plot.

The setting: a patchwork of what was
field tilting down towards beck, rising
again, to Killinghall and moor. As big a
sweep of sky as you can get. Survivor

of time and all weathers; square of
possibility, bequeathed in (good) will,
jealously overlooked by houses, roads,
backyards for being what it is: old soil.
Blessed. Left alone through centuries to
tick over to the rhythm of that old chant:
dig, turn, manure, break, plant,
water, weed, pick, rot. The soil begrudges
not the cast of beetles, worms, spiders,
frogs, slugs, snails. Or ancient ancestries
of rats and wood pigeons; it welcomes back
the time-slip kites, the fox-in-heat nights.
The frenzies of birth and death, the seeds,
yellow teeth and bones of long-ago devoured cows.
What a strange and familiar home this is, split
by its rickety barricades; conjoined by bedroom shelves,
seventies bathtubs, reclaimed floors, filing cabinets,
front doors. The make-do-and-mend philosophy
of prehistory. Enough junk to make good fences.
Enough air, space and luminous living
things to feed a family; to spark and fire the senses.

Some days a riot. Some days frozen, eerie quiet.
But a ragged tribe at work, always. A moan, nod
or *'Hello! How's it going? What've you got?*
D'you want to swap?' Or some seeds going spare
that you can't refuse or pay for, or a bumper crop
left anonymously by the compost. Or a hand to lend.

And now and then, a can of beer at very end of day.
Summer sunset; a shared, looking away to the west.
Rooks; swifts scrambling up to sky nests. Today:
a woman repairing a greenhouse, twins in tow,
humouring the old man and his unrequired advice
because she knows he's really aching for a daughter,
gone to live in Australia and there's no one home.
The new widow who gave us raspberry ripple apples
by the bucket that first year, in a headscarf; a lad who
smokes weed in his shed while he makes raised beds
for the ladies opposite, who are always impeccably
dressed and sometimes, subtly, hold hands. And the
couple from Ghana who grow tall, succulent corn
like you've never tasted. All these people rooted
in messy rows of chard and spinach and strawberries
and potatoes. All poised now like me, sweaty and red,
leaning on a spade with dirt smeared across my forehead
watching the sky catching light. Aching, but content.
And not one of us knows the time, or cares.

For eight years a man patiently tilled the plot
next to mine. A grey-haired Mauritian;
a nurse at the hospital who, post-shift,
nursed this earth. A man of luxuriant stories
and recipes. Spice insights: *You must dry-fry
in batches. Try! Promise me!*' He brought found
things for the children to collect: pennies, bent pins,
a key, buttons and clay pipes. Handfuls of clay pipes.

'They must have smoked all the time those bloody Victorians!'
Once he disappeared for a while. Months. His absence
registered in the bolted pak choi and unruly weeds.
The ground resented his wayward affection; it threw up
groundsel, dandelion and sow thistle with shocking speed.
I became worried, and aware of how deeply I cared.
Enquiries met shrugs, head shakes. Out of friendship
I appeased the season making a petulant point on his patch.
I tidied dwarf beans, watered when needed and almost
wept when I came down one morning and found him
lounging in a chair. *'I've been back home!'* He laughed.
'The sun! The sun there . . .' And so I thought nothing
when it happened again some months later. But then
his cousin, with a plot down the other end of the site,
was there one day wondering if I'd help clear his shed.
'Didn't you hear?' he said, tears rising at my confusion.
'He left us. Three weeks ago. He went in the night.'

When heart-sore, I often wonder if this place is
secretly a model for what should be; how things could be,
were we not so preoccupied with property:
the space to be alone, yet many; to work the small
corners in unity. To be granted parity from the off;
where difference is welcomed for its new thoughts, fruits,
new perspectives, new voices adding new depths to the old
chants. Where the chance to be author of our own fate is
grasped with both hands. Life in common, a law beholden
to land, season and locality, governed by the health of the

soil and each another. Oh, there'd be fierce competition still,
we're human after all, but where winning might mean
sharing. Earning the right to brag, but where prizes are
bagged and left by the gate with flowers for new arrivals.
We're given such scant measures. So few years in the sun.
Such poor odds. And we're the privileged ones, arriving
without the press of brutality or cruel legacy, or ground
ravaged by drought and war. Even then, life is fragile and
gossamer-thin. No sooner are we through the gate, narrowing
our eyes into wind, than we're mediating: *Let THIS seed grow,
please, not these weeds. Spare us from frost and disease.*
'Word to the wise,' a man once told me, handing over beans,
'Plant three: one for the birds, one for the earth, one for thee.
Then get on tha' knees and attend to what comes up tirelessly.'
Maybe that's the truce we need to reach. Or the harmony.

For one evening, too soon, the gate will be open.
We'll notice day has darkened, the sunset gone
behind the hill. And just as we're wondering,
who's that been left for? A voice on the wind
will start to whisper: *Come on, now. Come on.*
Someone else's turn. We'll hear the old chant:
dig, turn, manure, break, plant, water, weed,
pick, rot . . . and realise the flowers have been
left not for those arriving, but those leaving.
And we'll wish we had one more season to
witness perfection, but somewhere a bell will
be ringing and we'll already be walking home.

ABOUT THE CONTRIBUTORS

Jenny Chamarette is a queer non-binary writer, researcher, curator, artist and allotmenteer from south-east London who took on an allotment plot in autumn 2019, shortly before the outbreak of the Covid pandemic. Jenny has lived for many years with chronic illness and found writing and nature connection to be sources of truth in troubling times. *Q is for Garden*, Jenny's nature memoir, was shortlisted for the Nature Chronicles biennial prize 2021/2, the Fitzcarraldo Essay Prize 2021, and longlisted for the Nan Shepherd Prize 2021. An extract from *Q is for Garden* was published by Saraband in 2022. Elsewhere Jenny's public words have appeared with *MAI Journal, Another Gaze, Club des Femmes Culture Club*, LUX, *Litro Magazine, Sight & Sound* and recently in an artist's book by the queer art collective the Hildegard von Bingen Society for Gardening Companions.

Rob Cowen is an award-winning writer, hailed as one of the UK's most original voices on nature, place and people. His second book, *Common Ground* (PRH, 2015), was shortlisted for the Portico, Richard Jefferies Society and Wainwright prizes and voted one of the nation's favourite nature books of all time in a BBC poll. His follow-up, *The Heeding*, was the bestselling debut book of poetry in 2021 and his poems have featured on *Caught by the River* and in *Letters to the Earth* (HarperCollins). His forthcoming book, *NORTH ROAD* (PRH, 2025), is the epic and haunting story of a journey by foot over many years along the A1, the Great North Road, tracing this timeline from beginning to end. A genre-defying work, it blends memoir, history, fiction and short story to create a book that weaves time, place, memory and profound personal revelation written in dazzling prose. Rob lives in North Yorkshire.

Marchelle Farrell is a writer, medical psychotherapist and amateur gardener born in Trinidad and Tobago, who has spent over twenty years attempting to become hardy here in the UK. She is curious about the relationship between our external and internal landscapes, the patterns we re-enact in relation to the land, and how they might be changed. Her debut book, *Uprooting*, won the Nan Shepherd Prize for nature writing and is published by Canongate.

Olia Hercules is a British Ukrainian cookbook author, chef and activist. She has written four cookbooks, including award-winning *Mamushka*, which has been translated into eleven languages. Her third cookbook, *Summer Kitchens*, documents Ukrainian regional cuisine and preservation traditions. She is a co-founder of the movement Cook for Ukraine, which has helped to raise over £2 million for those affected by the war in Ukraine. Olia lives in London with her husband Joe and two young sons. She continues writing and raising awareness about Ukrainian culture.

David Keenan is the multi-award-winning author of six novels, including *This Is Memorial Device* and *Monument Maker*.

Heather Leigh is a musician, artist and gardener living in Glasgow, Scotland.

Kirsteen McNish is a writer whose creative work intersects with people, place, landscape and unusual settings, as well as encompassing caring and lesser-heard voices through the prism of the natural world. Kirsteen writes a regular column for *Caught by the River* and contributes to *Hole & Corner* among other publications.

JC Niala is an allotment historian and writer with a passion for exploring the intersection of nature, culture and community through the lens of allotments. Her doctoral research included thirty-six months of research on allotments and urban gardening sites in Oxford. Through this, she conceptualised allotments as banal utopias, everyday sanctuaries, where people collaboratively craft paradise with nature. She was awarded the Social History Society Public History Prize in 2022 for the recreation of an allotment in the style of the year 1918, which culminated in site events, exhibitions and the publication of an artist's journal of poems, *Portal: 1918 Allotment*. Her 2023 project was 'The Waiting List' – a collaboration between her artist collective and Greenpeace. Following conducting Freedom of Information requests to councils nationwide, they unveiled a massive allotment-sized artwork crafted from seed paper, stating, 'We the 174,183 on the waiting list demand allotments.' This was performed at the Department for Levelling Up, Housing and Communities, drawing attention to the lengthy waiting lists and illuminating the potential of allotments to sustain urban populations.

Graeme Rigby has written, performed, published and produced plays, poetry, documentary texts, a novel, music theatre, radio comedy and fish-based documentary. For eight years he edited *The Page*, an arts and literature paper for the North and for nineteen years was a member of Amber Film & Photography Collective. In 1991/92, he and the photographer Peter Fryer were commissioned by Newcastle upon Tyne City Council to explore allotment garden culture in the city, culminating in a book and exhibition called *Peaceable Kingdoms*. These days he restricts himself to writing the online *Rigby's Encyclopaedia of the Herring* at www.herripedia.com.

Rebecca Schiller is a writer and author of several non-fiction books including *Earthed* and *Amazing Activists*. She is co-founder of the human rights charity Birthrights, runs Mothers Who Write, and her journalism has appeared in a range of publications including the *Observer*. Rebecca lives on a croft in the north-east of Scotland with her family and animals.

Sui Searle is a gardener, writer and printmaker. She retrained in horticulture as a career change and has worked in botanic, public, private and community gardens as well as spending a short period writing for gardening magazines. She is the founder of @decolonise thegarden (https://www.instagram.com/decolonisethegarden/), which focuses on bringing a decolonial lens to horticulture, and is editor of the alternative online gardening newsletter, Radicle (http://radicle.substack.com/). Both aim to seek, in community, possibilities of an otherwise. She sees the garden as a site of ever-changing co-creation with the potential to practise other modes of being – a place to practise being in kinship and cultivating deeper relationships with our more-than-human kin.

Sara Venn is a horticulturalist and social and environmental activist. She is the founder of Edible Bristol, a community-led organisation that supports people and communities to grow on lost and unloved pieces of land, and is often described as someone who 'gets shit done'. Sara is passionate about sharing her skills to create resilience in communities, and to make food growing and gardening accessible to all. She has been growing in allotments since childhood: they are the places where her theoretical knowledge became her practical understanding of the importance of getting our hands in the soil and connecting with food and nature.

Alice Vincent (@alicevincentwrites) is a writer, broadcaster and the author of three books, including the bestselling *Why Women Grow: Stories of Soil, Sisterhood and Survival*, which was shortlisted for the 2023 Books Are My Bag Readers Awards, and *Rootbound: Rewilding a Life*. Both were longlisted for the Wainwright Prize. A self-taught gardener, Alice is a columnist for the *Guardian* and *Gardens Illustrated* and writes for titles including *Vogue* and the *New Statesman*. She has been documenting her gardening online since 2015 and has since launched a newsletter and podcast. She lives in south London.

ABOUT THE EDITOR

Sarah Rigby is an editor, publisher and book coach, and publishing director at the vibrant independent Elliott & Thompson. She has published some of the country's best-loved and award-winning writers of nature and place, including Nancy Campbell, Rob Cowen and James Aldred. Originally from Yorkshire, she lives in London with her family, where she shares an allotment with her friend Viv and volunteers for Organic Lea, a workers' co-operative and community food-growing project on the edge of Epping Forest.